INSIGHT GUIDES

GLASGOW

POCKET GUIDE

PLAN & BOOK
YOUR TAILOR-MADE TRIP

BRAZIL

CHILE

ECUADOR

TAILOR-MADE TRIPS & UNIQUE EXPERIENCES CREATED BY LOCAL TRAVEL EXPERTS AT INSIGHTGUIDES.COM/HOLIDAYS

Insight Guides has been inspiring travellers with high-quality travel content for over 45 years. As well as our popular guidebooks, we now offer the opportunity to book tailor-made private trips completely personalised to your needs and interests. By connecting with one of our local experts, you will directly benefit from their expertise and local know-how, helping you create memories that will last a lifetime.

HOW INSIGHTGUIDES.COM/HOLIDAYS WORKS

STEP 1

Pick your dream destination and submit an enquiry, or modify an existing itinerary if you prefer.

STEP 2
Fill in a short form, sharing details of your travel plans and preferences with a local expert.

STEP 3

Your local expert will create your personalised itinerary, which you can amend until you are completely satisfied.

STEP 4

Book securely online. Pack your bags and enjoy your holiday! Your local expert will be available to answer questions during your trip.

BENEFITS OF PLANNING & BOOKING AT INSIGHTGUIDES.COM/HOLIDAYS

PLANNED BY LOCAL EXPERTS
The Insight Guides local experts are hand-picked, based on their experience in the travel industry and their impeccable standards of customer service.

SAVE TIME & MONEY
When a local expert plans your trip, you save time and money when you book, even during high season. You won't be charged for using a credit card either.

TAILOR-MADE TRIPS
Book with Insight Guides, and you will be in complete control of the planning process, from the initial selections to amending your final itinerary.

BOOK & TRAVEL STRESS-FREE
Enjoy stress-free travel when you use the Insight Guides secure online booking platform. All bookings come with a money-back guarantee.

WHAT OTHER TRAVELLERS THINK ABOUT TRIPS BOOKED AT INSIGHTGUIDES.COM/HOLIDAYS

Trip to Vietnam

The organization was superb, the drivers professional, and accommodation quite comfortable. I was well taken care of! My thanks to your colleagues who helped make my trip to Vietnam such a great experience. My only regret is that I couldn't spend more time in the country.

Heather   ★★★★★

DON'T MISS OUT
BOOK NOW AT
INSIGHTGUIDES.COM/HOLIDAYS

TOP 10 ATTRACTIONS

KELVINGROVE PARK
Quintessential Victorian park and the Kelvingrove Art Gallery. See page 56.

CHARLES RENNIE MACKINTOSH
Pioneer of the modernist movement. See page 48.

CULTURE AND NIGHTLIFE
Cutting-edge theatre, bustling arts centres, lively music venues and nightspots to suit all tastes. See page 85.

GLASGOW CATHEDRAL
A 12th-century cathedral surrounded by the city's oldest buildings and the burial site of St Mungo. See page 29.

WHISKY
Distilleries overlooking the Clyde and numerous bars filled to the rafters with whisky. See page 104.

UNIVERSITY OF GLASGOW
Captivating cloisters and imaginative exhibitions at the university's Hunterian Museum. See page 60.

GEORGE SQUARE
Space to relax, surrounded by prime shopping and dining. See page 44.

SCOTTISH FOOTBALL
Old Firm rivalries, international matches and plenty of great teams make Glasgow the home of Scottish football. See page 88.

RIVERSIDE MUSEUM
Family-friendly transport museum in Zaha Hadid's impressive riverside building. See page 67.

LOCH LOMOND
The jewel of the Trossachs, surrounded by pretty villages and hiking trails. See page 77.

A PERFECT DAY

9.00am

Glasgow Necropolis
Get a sense of Glasgow's rich past as well as a good view of the city from the vantage point of the Glasgow Necropolis. Wander among the tombs of the city's revered past citizens and keep an eye out for tombs designed by Charles Rennie Mackintosh, Alexander 'Greek' Thompson and others.

10.30am

Tron Gate
Discover Victorian Glasgow in the form of the grand monuments and statues on Glasgow Green and learn about the city's industrial past at the People's Palace. Stop for a cup of tea in the museum café or grab a pint in one of Glasgow's oldest pubs, The Saracen Head, on Gallowgate.

12.00pm

Explore Merchant City
Cross over from Tron Gate into the dynamic and historic Merchant Quarter, past the old 18th century sandstone buildings and warehouses that have been transformed into gin bars, glamorous restaurants, stylish boutiques and concept stores. Look out for the huge Badminton, Billy Connolly and Fellow Glasgow Residents murals that adorn several buildings.

1.30pm

Lunch
Have a burger heaped high with fillings at Maggie Mays or stop in at one of the cafes of Merchant City, like McCune Smith, for a craft coffee and a light bite to fuel up for the second half of the day. Then head towards Glasgow Central, stopping in at the Gallery of Modern Art on the way.

IN GLASGOW

4.30pm

Wander along the Clyde
Follow the riverside path west along the north bank of the Clyde past iconic modern riverside monuments like the Clyde Arc and SEC Armadillo. Cross the river at Bell's Bridge to see traditional steamships like the PS *Waverley*, the last sea-going paddle steamer in the world, moored to the quay beside the Science Centre.

9.00pm

'Glesga' nightlife
Sample Scotland's finest clubbing scene at a city centre venue like Sub Club. Alternatively, catch a live theatrical performance at one of Glasgow's many theatres, or some live music at Òran Mór in the West End or the Glasgow Royal Concert Hall. There are plenty of smaller gigs at various pubs across the city too.

3.00pm

Shopping in Glasgow Central
Start out in George Square, surrounded by its grand public buildings, and indulge in some shopping at Princes Square Shopping Centre and along Buchanan Street before heading to the Willow Tea Rooms, its exquisite interiors designed by Charles Rennie Mackintosh, for afternoon tea.

7.00pm

Dinner in the West End
Begin your evening with a tipple in The Ben Nevis, a traditional Glaswegian pub with occasional live folk music. Then pick from among a fine selection of restaurants along Argyle Street or around Byres Road in Glasgow's lively West End to sample some classic Scottish fare.

CONTENTS

INTRODUCTION

Scotland's largest metropolitan area, and very much the country's phoenix from the flames, Glasgow is an upbeat city that has undergone a number of transformative identity changes throughout its history. Encountering both grit and finesse in equal measure, you can learn a lot about this city's highs and lows just by wandering along the undulating streets of its centre. From ecclesiastical beginnings, Glasgow swelled in size and strategic importance during the Industrial Revolution, thanks to its position on the banks of the mighty River Clyde, which empties out into the sea 26 miles to the west. When heavy industries began to decline in the mid-20th century, however, Glasgow was plunged into an era of poverty and unemployment, along with all the attendant social ills that go with them. But all the while, a proud cultural legacy endured, leading to the city being awarded the European Capital of Culture status in 1990. This significant turning point brings us to today, where, following a prolonged phase of regeneration, Glasgow is again considered to be one of Europe's most significant hubs of, among other things, architecture, sport and culture.

ONE CITY, TWO HALVES

Located on the western side of Scotland's Central Belt – on the opposite side of which you'll find the capital city, Edinburgh, 45 miles away – Glasgow is spread across the broad alluvial plain of the Clyde, which bisects the city right down the middle. This river has been both the making and breaking of the city; first it was the access point for tobacco ships coming from the Americas, before facilitating the heavy industries of chemicals, textiles and shipbuilding.

Particularly during the Victorian era, much of this rapid influx of wealth was parlayed into museums like Kelvingrove and the People's Palace, wide streets lined by sandstone townhouses, and fine municipal buildings, most of which were built north of the river. The demand for stately architecture opened the door to the emergence of an architectural movement befitting this new wealth.

The distinctive outline of the Campsie Fells

Cue Charles Rennie Mackintosh, a pioneer of the modernist movement, although his work displays more artistry than the utilitarianism for which modernism later became known. Mackintosh was greatly influenced by Art Nouveau as well as by nature, much of which can still be enjoyed around the city. North of Glasgow the plains break into the Campsie Fells, which give way to the beautiful green expanse of the Trossachs National Park, containing Loch Lomond. These areas make for excellent excursions from the city, and can be reached in well under an hour by car.

The south bank of the River Clyde presents a different story. It is mainly residential, with large tenement blocks built to house the city's large workforce during the industrial era and beyond. When heavy industry declined, so too did the living standards of the workers, who found themselves unemployed and poorly supported by the state. The banks of the River Clyde became a wasteland of empty warehouses and disused dry docks. These areas of deprivation have become the focus of much regeneration in the last three decades, and the Clyde is now home to some of the most ambitious modern architecture in Britain, including the Riverside Museum, designed by Zaha Hadid, and the reflective carapace of the Science Museum, which sits across from the collection of SEC entertainment complex buildings, that include the Norman Foster-designed Armadillo. All of this forms part of a larger urban renewal project in the city that has attracted over £5 billion of public and private investment, with more plans in development, suggesting that Glasgow's skyline may host more iconic buildings in the decades to come.

CULTURAL CAPITAL

One of the biggest draws for visitors to Glasgow today is its immensely vibrant cultural scene. Theatres, festivals, music venues and cinemas are plentiful throughout the city centre and beyond. The Glasgow School of Art is so highly-regarded that two fires which gutted the building in 2014 and again in 2018 were considered national tragedies. More recently, street art and vast murals have started to appear, particularly around Merchant City. The Gallery of Modern Art champions local contemporary artists, while the Burrell Collection houses one of the finest exhibitions of art in Europe. The European Capital of Culture may only be gifted to a city for a year, but in Glasgow it has endured well into its fourth decade with no sign of slowing down.

Two of Glasgow's great organisations showcasing nationally-prestigious culture are the Scottish National Ballet, which has a base at the Tramway arts space south of the Clyde, and the Scottish National Opera, headquartered at the Theatre Royal. The Tron, King's, and Pavilion theatres all have excellent stage-based schedules throughout the year. High art of a musical variety can also be found at the Glasgow Royal Concert Hall and the BBC's Scottish Symphony Orchestra is usually found in the City Halls & Old Fruitmarket. The gig scene in Glasgow is also thriving, with local bands playing at a multitude of venues around the city, such as Barrowlands Ballroom. Oasis are even said to have been discovered in the revered King Tut's Wah Wah Hut.

Festivals are commonplace in Glasgow, with international jazz, science and music events held annually, along with more esoteric festivities like the National Pipe Band Championships. Every two years, the Glasgow Biennale commandeers the city centre in a celebration of all things contemporary art. Usually taking place over three weeks from late April to mid-May, it's a fine showcase of Glasgow's thriving arts scene.

Celtic Connections Festival at The Old Fruit Market

PEOPLE MAKE GLASGOW

People make Glasgow what it is, something that is not lost on the city's authorities whose 'People Make Glasgow', campaign is now the city's official marketing slogan. Behind all of the city's creativity, an ever-growing number of eminent Glaswegians in intellectual and creative arenas are making significant contributions to the fields of global medicine, chemistry, technology, industry, science, and the arts. Sport should not be forgotten either. Football is a second religion to most Glaswegians, with five major teams in the metropolitan area, not least the Old Firm clubs of Celtic and Rangers. Meanwhile Scotland's national stadium, Hampden Park, is also located in Glasgow. In 2014 the city became the centre of international focus once again as it hosted the Commonwealth Games, and it has been selected as one of the host cities for the European Football Championships in 2020. Southwest of the city, around Prestwick, you'll find some very important golf clubs, including the Royal Troon, where the Open Championship is frequently held.

⊘ RAISING A LAUGH

Glaswegians stereotypically have a way with words, even if visitors have difficulty understanding them. The patter, sociologists argue, is a mix of native sharpness, Highland feyness, Jewish morbidity and the Irish *craic* (witty storytelling). Much of Glasgow's story has involved harsh or difficult living conditions, and raising a laugh serves as an antidote to adversity. The shipyards of the 1960s and 1970s, for example, provided plenty of material for Glaswegian comedian, Billy Connolly.

Enjoying the sun in George Square

You'll likely encounter many versions of Glasgow though on your trip: the modern face of the city is best represented in the hip West End, with a slew of stylish designer bars opening up, and a culinary renaissance sweeping through the city's excellent restaurants, craft coffee houses, and independent brewery taprooms.

To the east of the city centre you'll discover a Glasgow that was one of the earliest Catholic hubs in Scotland, while the Victorian legacy can be found in various public parks, often accompanied by grand edifices housing impressive selections of historical artefacts or works of art. And around Glasgow Central, old buildings have been converted into shopping centres, pubs, fancy hotels and modern office spaces. Here you are most likely to see the city's latest development under way; a sign that Glasgow is still an evolving place, busy writing the next chapter of its fascinating story, and one which is a joy to witness at every level.

A BRIEF HISTORY

In 2009, archaeologists discovered flint arrowheads placing the first human activity in the Glasgow and Clyde region as far back as the 12th century BC. As the receding Ice Age ushered in the Holocene, hunters followed game, namely wild horses and reindeer, ever further north. However, it is thought that there was no regular settlement in the Clyde area until around 4000 BC.

Little is known about the inhabitants of Scotland before the Romans arrived. The empire advanced north of the present-day border between England and Scotland, but only held the land around Glasgow for a few decades. The Romans never

⊙ ROMAN GLASGOW

The mighty Roman Empire swelled to include much of Britain, but crashed up against Caledonia (Scotland) in around AD 71, struggling to make any lasting breakthrough. Although watchtowers and outposts were set up around present-day Glasgow, the empire's official north-western frontier became the Antonine Wall in AD 142, when Emperor Antoninus Pius ordered a wall built across the Central Belt (between the firths of Forth and Clyde). Constructed mainly of turf, with a number of forts and outposts stationed along its length, the Antonine Wall only stayed in Roman hands for four decades, before they fell back to the better-fortified Hadrian's Wall. Today the Antonine Wall's remnants can best be appreciated at Bar Hill Fort and the Bearsden Bathhouse, both of which are a 30-minute drive from central Glasgow. The best collection of Scotland's Roman artefacts is housed in the Hunterian Museum.

gained overall control of Scotland, and their final retreat led to centuries of turmoil between warring tribes of Scots, Picts, Britons and Angles from the 3rd century AD.

A PLACE OF PILGRIMAGE

A Gaelic-speaking tribe from Ireland, the Scots founded a shaky kingdom in Argyll, to the west of Glasgow, known as 'Dalriada'. In the late 4th

The remains of the Roman Antonine Wall

century a Scot, St Ninian, travelled to Rome and, on his return to Strathclyde, introduced Christianity to Scotland. But it is Kentigern (later known as St Mungo) who is credited as the founder of Glasgow in c. 543, although only legend bears witness to his arrival. The city's name is said to derive from the Celtic *Glas-cu*, which loosely translates as 'the dear, green place'.

Glasgow Cathedral was founded in 1136 on the site of St Mungo's Church, beside the Molendinar, a pretty *burn* (stream) that was covered over in the 1870s. Pilgrims were soon drawn to St Mungo's shrine, which led to the establishment of an archbishopric, and city status, in 1492. However, it was the founding of the University of Glasgow in 1451 that brought the city the most prestige towards the end of the Middle Ages. By 1560 the Scottish Reformation had officially ended Catholicism in Glasgow, so the city's outward importance continued primarily due to its Clyde River bridge crossing and education facilities.

Tobacco trade

In 1738 Scotland's share of the tobacco trade, based in Glasgow, was 10 percent; by 1769 it was more than 52 percent.

TOBACCO AND COTTON

While Edinburgh had long been Scotland's most important seat of power, Glasgow's importance as a commercial and industrial hub was only realised in the 18th century, thanks to growing transatlantic trade, coupled with the technological developments that ushered in the Industrial Revolution. The burgeoning British Empire spawned Glasgow's growth as an important port city because the Clyde was a large, navigable river which provided a shorter passage to the Americas than other British cities.

The first cargo of tobacco from Virginia arrived in Glasgow in 1674; thirty years later, the 1707 Act of Union between Scotland and England – unpopular in Glasgow – led to a boom in trade with the colonies. In the 1770s the ingenious plan of civil engineers John and James Golborne to build piers along the banks of the Clyde turned Glasgow into a serious contender as an Atlantic port.

Glasgow's tobacco monopoly enriched its 'Tobacco Lords', who were the city's first major merchants. Many of their houses still stand. They created not only the tobacco trade with Maryland, Virginia and North Carolina, but also a merchant class in Glasgow. This stimulated Scottish manufacturing, which thrived under the terms of the Navigation Acts, whereby Americans were not allowed to trade manufactured goods. As such, Scottish-produced linen, paper and wrought iron were exchanged for Virginia tobacco.

When the American War of Independence disrupted trade in the 1770s and 1780s, the Scots successfully turned to trade with the West Indies and, most important of all, to the production of cotton. Glasgow soon became a cotton city. Within a decade, scores of mills were using the fast-flowing Scottish rivers to power their looms. In 1787, Scotland had only 19 textile mills; by 1840 there were nearly 200.

INDUSTRIAL PURPOSE

By the middle of the 19th century, Glasgow's enormous industrial vitality was evident. The extensive use of steam power created a massive demand for coal from the abundant coalfields of nearby Lanarkshire. This once-small Georgian city had become a huge industrial metropolis built on the kind of rectangular grid common in the United States, with industrial princes living in splendour while Highland, Irish, Italian and Jewish immigrants languished in the deprived slums.

Other industries began to flourish, like the metal-bashing industries – shipbuilding, ironworks and armaments – which were complemented by textiles, chemicals and manufacturing. For generations the label 'Clyde built' was synonymous with industrial quality. Scotland's shipbuilding industry had begun as early as 1802, when the steam vessel *Charlotte Dundas* was launched on the Forth

Sorting tobacco leaves at the Three Nuns factory

Population boom

Glasgow's population grew from 23,500 in 1755 to 200,000 in 1840, at which point it exploded, doubling to 400,000 by 1870. It reached a peak of 1,128,000 in 1939. Today the city holds roughly 630,000 inhabitants, with 1,655,000 people living in the wider metropolitan area.

and Clyde Canal. But by the turn of the twentieth century, most industries had been honed into one massive shipbuilding culture. Everything from tugboats to transatlantic liners was fashioned out of sheet metal in the yards that straddled the Clyde from Gourock to Rutherglen.

VICTORIAN GLASGOW AND BUST

The Victorian age transformed Glasgow beyond recognition. The population mushroomed to nearly 800,000 at the end of the 19th century, and new tenement blocks swept into the suburbs in an attempt to cope with the influx of people. At this time Glasgow revelled in the title of the 'Second City of the Empire', an unexpected epithet for a place that rarely acknowledges second place in anything.

Two vast and stately International Exhibitions were held in 1888 and 1901 to showcase the city and its industries to the outside world, necessitating the construction of huge civic monoliths such as the Kelvingrove Art Gallery and the Council Chambers in George Square. This channelling of the wealth into culture and architecture sowed the seeds of Glasgow's present-day revival, not that the city's late-nineteenth-century inhabitants would ever have conceived of a downturn in their fortunes: the well-paid Clydeside engineers went to their forges wearing bowler hats and starched collars. They were confident but their optimism was misplaced.

Scotland's industries were very much geared to the export market, and after World War I, conditions were much changed. During the war, when exports had been curtailed by a combination of U-boat activity and war production, new industries had developed in India and Japan, and the eastern market for Scottish goods never recovered. The post-war world also witnessed a contraction of world trade, which hit the shipbuilding industry very hard and, in turn, damaged the steel and coal industries.

These difficulties were compounded by the financial collapse of the early 1930s, and by 1932, 28 percent of the Scottish workforce was unemployed. Some 400,000 Scots emigrated between 1921 and 1931, and those who stayed endured some of the worst social conditions in the British Isles. By the late

The Central Hall at the Glasgow International Exhibition of 1888

1930s, Scotland had the highest infant mortality rate in Europe. High unemployment remained, although there was a partial economic recovery in the mid-1930s, it was curtailed by the start of World War II.

RENAISSANCE

Shipbuilding, and many associated industries, died away almost completely in the 1960s and 1970s, leaving the city depressed, jobless and directionless. The only ray of light for many locals was the city's footballing prowess, as Celtic won the European Cup in 1967, becoming the first British team to do so. Rangers followed this up by triumphing in the UEFA European Cup Winner's Cup in 1972.

⊙ THE IMPACT OF INDUSTRY

Heavy industry made Glasgow and heavy industry eventually broke it. People started to flock to the 'Workshop of the British Empire'. Such sudden growth created urban overcrowding on a massive scale and, as late as 1861, 64 percent of the entire population lived in cramped one- or two-room tenement houses. Working-class conditions were appalling. Rickets, cholera, smallpox, tuberculosis, diphtheria and alcoholism were rampant. The streets were unclean and unsafe; violence was endemic. Yet while the work was there, people kept coming. In the harsh economic climate of the 1930s, however, factories closed, unemployment spiralled, and Glasgow could do little to counter its image as a city dominated by inebriate violence and sectarian tensions between Catholics and Protestants. The Gorbals area in particular became notorious as one of the worst slums in Europe.

The 2014 Commonwealth Games in the SSE Hydro

In the 1980s Glasgow's rebranding began, starting with the upbeat 'Glasgow's Miles Better' campaign in 1983, gathering pace towards the 1988 Garden Festival and the year-long party as European Capital of Culture in 1990. Further prestige came in 1999 when Glasgow was designated UK City of Architecture and Design. The city has since gone on to host a number of big events: the 2002 Champions' League Final, the 2014 Commonwealth Games and the 2019 European Athletics Indoor Championships. These various titles have helped to reinforce the impression that Glasgow, despite its many problems, has successfully broken the industrial shackles of the past and evolved into a city of stature, modernity and confidence.

REFERENDA AND FUTURE PROSPECTS

In 1997 the Scots voted overwhelmingly for the re-establishment of a Scottish Parliament. This new Parliament, which opened in 1999, gained control over all local affairs, such as education, economic development, agriculture and the environment, but with a limited ability to collect and control tax revenues. Nonetheless, many Scots saw this as a new beginning, a chance to assert their national identity and protect their culture and heritage.

Brexit sign in Glasgow Central station

In the Scottish Independence referendum of September 2014 some of the most deprived neighbourhoods in Glasgow voted overwhelmingly for independence. The referendum had an energising effect on the political scene in Scotland and politicised a whole new generation. Nevertheless, the Scottish people as a whole voted to stay within the United Kingdom by 55 to 45 percent.

Then in 2016 came the 'Brexit' referendum, in which 52 percent of UK voters opted to leave the EU, though in Scotland 62 percent voted to remain in the EU, prompting many within the SNP to call for another independence referendum. At the time of writing there had been repeated delays to the Brexit date and no real indication of when or how the UK was going to leave the European Union, and the very real possibility of the break-up of the union looming on the horizon.

Glasgow's recent city administrations have pragmatically courted private finance to unlock the city's post-industrial potential. New developments and regeneration projects have given the city a sense of civic pride. Around £5 billion of public and private investment has started to transform the once-bleak banks of the Clyde and Glasgow looks forward to a positive future as this forward-thinking continues.

HISTORICAL LANDMARKS

c. 12,000 BC Earliest known human activity in the Glasgow region.

AD 142 Romans begin building the Antonine Wall north of Glasgow.

c. 543 St Mungo (Kentigern) founds the city of Glasgow.

1136 Construction begins on Glasgow Cathedral.

1286 Glasgow gets its first wooden bridge over the Clyde.

1297 William Wallace begins his revolt, killing the English High Sheriff in Lanark.

1305 Wallace is captured at Robroyston, in the north of Glasgow, and executed in London.

1451 The University of Glasgow is founded.

1492 Glasgow becomes an archbishopric.

1568 Mary Queen of Scots forces lose the Battle of Langside.

1707 Act of Union between England and Scotland.

early-1700s The tobacco trade starts using Glasgow as a base.

1765 James Watt invents the steam engine.

1770 Civil engineers John and James Golborne build piers to scour the bed of the River Clyde, turning Glasgow into a serious contender as an Atlantic port.

1811 Glasgow becomes the second city of the British Empire.

1900 Glasgow is at the peak of its cultural and industrial production.

1940s Advent of decline as heavy industries start to close down.

1967 Celtic win the European Cup.

1972 Rangers win the UEFA European Cup Winner's Cup.

1990 Glasgow becomes the European Capital of Culture.

1997 Referendum votes in favour of separate Scottish Parliament.

2000 The Science Centre opens, sparking a rejuvenation along the Clyde.

2014 Scotland votes to stay within the United Kingdom. Glasgow hosts the Commonwealth Games.

2016 Scotland votes in favour of staying in the EU by 62 to 38 percent.

2018 Glasgow School of Art is devastated by fire for the second time in four years.

2019 One of Glasgow's last remaining shipyards is nationalised.

2020 Glasgow is a host city for the Euro Football Championships

The Bridge of Sighs, connecting
Cathedral Square and the Necropolis

WHERE TO GO

Glasgow enjoys a rich mix of traditional and contemporary neighbourhoods which combine various historic, cultural, gastronomic, architectural and educational experiences. Most are walkable. The Glasgow Subway links Buchanan Street to the West End. A good way to get the most from your visit is to divide the city into separate tours, allowing roughly half a day or more for each area. Open-top tour buses start in front of Merchant House on George Square and stop at many of the main sights covered in this book.

PRE-INDUSTRIAL GLASGOW

Although there is no accurate date for the first settlement of Glasgow, many believe that Kentigern's arrival in c. 543 heralded the beginning of the city's rise. While lacking the historical significance of Edinburgh – most of Glasgow's finest buildings date only as far back as the late 18th century – what is certain is that Catholicism gave the fledgling town purpose and fostered its growth.

CATHEDRAL SQUARE

The city's oldest buildings can be found around **Cathedral Square**, which is guarded by a rather imperious equestrian statue of William of Orange. It is said that the tail of 'King Billy's' horse was once broken off by a reveller (statues in Glasgow tend to receive a lot of after-hours attention) and replaced with a ball and socket joint, with the result that on particularly stormy days, the tail can be seen to wave in the breeze.

The oldest dwelling-house still standing in Glasgow is **Provand's Lordship ❶** (www.glasgowlife.org.uk; Tue–Thu & Sat 10am–5pm, Fri & Sun 11am–5pm; free). It lies opposite Cathedral Square and was built in 1471 by Bishop Andrew Muirhead to house the master of the hospice of St Nicholas. The house was saved and restored in 1906, with financial aid and period furnishings supplied by Sir William Burrell in 1927.

As a reminder of the manse's earthier history, the upper floor contains portraits of assorted characters such as the notorious drunkards and prostitutes of eighteenth- and nineteenth-century Glasgow; one of the most infamous being Hawkie, a street beggar and political street entertainer. Behind it lies a **Physic Garden**, in tribute to St Nicholas. The sound of the traffic gives way to medieval calm here, among the herb plantings and knot gardens. Behind the wall, towards the Strathclyde campus, is a small but ambitious orchard.

Back across Castle Street – traffic is always bad here – is the **St Mungo Museum of Religious Life and Art ❷** (www.glasgow life.org.uk; Tue–Thu & Sat 10am–5pm, Fri & Sun 11am–5pm; free). The honey-coloured stone building stands on the site of the medieval Bishop's Castle and houses works of art from the main world religions – Buddhist, Muslim, Christian, Hindu, Jewish and Sikh – as well as from many minor ones. Inside there are powerful images of religious figures and rites to explore, including an imposing bronze sculpture of the Hindu god Shiva, Lord of the Dance, and a Mexican Day of the Dead skeleton, which celebrates the victory of life over death. Illuminating the fascinating artworks are some stunning stained-glass windows depicting Christian saints and prophets. The museum's pleasant coffee shop backs onto an attractive Zen-style garden designed by Yasutaro Tanaka – another unexpected haven of peace on this busy street.

Provand's Lordship

The cathedral precinct is fronted by a statue of the Scottish missionary explorer David Livingstone and provides an excellent foreground for the massive bulk of the **Glasgow Royal Infirmary**, which commemorates the 65-year reign of Queen Victoria. The 'Royal', which has been operating since 1794, has made a proud contribution to world medicine: Lord Lister pioneered antiseptic surgery here in the 1860s; Sir William Macewen established his reputation in brain surgery and osteopathy here in the 1890s; and his matron Mrs Rebecca Strong introduced the world's first systematic training for nurses.

GLASGOW CATHEDRAL

At the east end of the precinct lies **Glasgow Cathedral** ❸ (www.glasgowcathedral.org; Apr–Sept Mon–Sat 9.30am–5pm, Sun 1–4.30pm, Oct–Mar Mon–Sat 10am–3.30pm, Sun 1–3.30pm; free). The tides of history have washed over this important ecclesiastical site since Glasgow's early days. It was founded in 1136 on the site of St Mungo's Church and was not completed until the late 15th century, with the final reconstruction of the chapterhouse and the aisle commissioned by Robert Blacader, the city's first archbishop. It has long been a focus for Christian learning and culture in Scotland, and has stood through the supremacy of the bishops, the War of Independence, and the upheaval of the Reformation.

Because of the sloping ground on which it is built, at its east end the cathedral is configured on two levels, the crypt being part of the lower church. On either side of the nave, the narrow aisles are illuminated by vivid stained-glass windows from the 19th and 20th centuries, with two 21st century additions, the Millennium Window and the Tree of Jesse. Beyond

Glasgow Cathedral

the nave, there's a view of the choir ceiling. In the choir's northeastern corner, a small door leads into the sacristy, in which the University of Glasgow was founded over 500 years ago. Wooden boards on the walls detail the clergy of the cathedral in chronological order, from Catholic to Protestant to the Church of Scotland.

Two sets of steps from the nave lead down into the lower church, where you'll find a dark and musty chapel that surrounds the tomb of St Mungo, although the saint's relics were removed in the late Middle Ages and their whereabouts is now unknown. The chapel itself is one of the most glorious examples of medieval architecture in Scotland, best seen in the delicate fan vaulting that rises up from a thicket of cool stone columns.

Other intriguing architectural and social developments occurred after the Reformation and allowed three different congregations to worship in separate spaces within the cathedral, reflecting rank and class divisions. From 1595, the Barony Parishioners worshipped in the lower church (crypt), while from 1648 the High Kirk congregation worshipped in the choir itself, and the nave was used by worshippers from the eastern part of the city. Blue-robed custodians belonging to the Society of Friends of Glasgow Cathedral give fascinating impromptu tours from Monday to Saturday.

THE NECROPOLIS

Rising up behind the cathedral, the atmospheric **Necropolis** ❹ (www.glasgownecropolis.org; daily 7am–dusk; free) is a grassy mound covered in a fantastic assortment of crumbling gravestones, ornate urns, gloomy catacombs and neoclassical temples. It was inspired by the Père Lachaise cemetery in Paris, and was established in 1832. From the summit, next to a column topped with an indignant John Knox, there are superb views of the cathedral below and the city beyond. Many of the monuments were designed by major architects and sculptors, including Alexander 'Greek' Thomson, **Charles Rennie Mackintosh** and J.T. Rochead, which makes a walk around the sprawling site a fascinating insight into both Victorian and Edwardian styles and tastes.

The administration and maintenance of the Necropolis was handed from Merchants' House to Glasgow City Council in 1966. Various paths lead through the rows of graves and mausolea, many of which have been refurbished under the guidance of The Friends of Glasgow Necropolis, a superb organisation which maps and restores the graves, runs tours of the site, and helps visitors locate ancestors who may have been interred here.

THE EAST END

Despite all the upbeat hype, Glasgow's gentrification has largely passed by many deprived inner-city areas including

⊘ THE NOTABLE INTERRED

The Necropolis quickly became a fitting spot for the great and the good of wealthy 19th century Glasgow to indulge their vanity; some 50,000 burials have taken place, and there are 3,500 monuments. Scientists, inventors, industrialists and architects are all commemorated, either directly through interment, or indirectly through the designs and architecture marking the tombs. It is believed that Charles Rennie Mackintosh's first recorded commission was for the design of a monument here in 1888, a tribute to the dead marking the birth of his career. His Celtic Cross denotes the resting place of Alexander McCall, formerly the Chief Constable of the Glasgow Police force, for whom Mackintosh's policeman father worked. Victorian death symbology is rife throughout the Necropolis: birds, palm branches, flying angels and burning torches all signify resurrection; a draped urn signifies mourning for an older person, while an undraped urn is mourning for a younger person; ivy and a snake biting its own tail represent immortality.

much of the **East End**. Indeed, even in the more fashionable quarters of Glasgow, there's a gritty edge that's never far away, reinforcing a peculiar mix of grime and glitz that the city seems to have patented. From the cathedral, High Street leads southwest, passing some fine redbrick tenements housing a curious assortment of stores, including the occult shop 23 Enigma. A couple of the finest murals

Apple Ale, brewed at the Drygate brewery

on Glasgow's **Mural Trail** (www.citycentremuraltrail.co.uk), such as the impossible to miss 'Saint Mungo', which fills an entire end-terrace wall, can be found around here.

THE BREWERIES

Head south from the cathedral on John Knox Street, however, and you will encounter a distinctive malty smell emanating from two of Glasgow's most popular breweries. Injecting a welcome dollop of life into the East End, **Drygate Brewery** (www.drygate.com; daily 11am–midnight, brewery tours: Sat 5pm & 7pm, Sun 1pm, 3pm & 5pm) is the smaller and newer of the two. This progressive brewery is housed in a converted box factory that is a nod to Glasgow's industrial past.

Heading East on Duke Street, you'll likely notice the huge steel tanks of the **Tennent's Wellpark Brewery ❺** (161 Duke St; www.tennentstours.com; tours: Mon–Sat hourly 11am–6pm

Civic punishment

If spirits haunt any part of Glasgow, it should be Mercat Cross. Men and women were hanged outside the Tolbooth Steeple, and alleged witches and miscreants scourged. The original building had spikes on the walls for the decapitated heads of felons.

Sun hourly noon–5pm), which supplies a commodity as welcome to many Glaswegians as Loch Katrine's water. This is a brewery on a much larger scale. The Tennent's Story Heritage Centre has a well-curated exhibition dedicated to the city's favourite beer, and the history of brewing on this site, dating back centuries. It is best explored before a brewery tour.

Mercat Cross is dominated by the **Tolbooth Steeple ❻**, which lies stranded in the middle of busy traffic where the High Street passes into Saltmarket. The Tolbooth was once an integral part of civic life in Glasgow and has occupied this site in various forms since the earliest days. Its functions were manifold, from a meeting place for the town council, to a tax collection point, courthouse and jail.

East of Mercat Cross, down Gallowgate beyond the train lines, lies the heart of the East End district, an area that perhaps most closely corresponds to the old perception of Glasgow. Hemmed in by Glasgow Green to the south and the old university to the west, this densely packed industrial area, with its isolated pubs, and tatty discount shops and cafés, stands in stark contrast to the glossy Merchant City only a few blocks to the west. But unless you're lost here after hours it's not threatening, and there's no doubt that the area offers a rich flavour of working-class Glasgow.

For example, the once-legendary East End ballroom, **Barrowland Ballroom ❼** (http://barrowland-ballroom.co.uk)

is a live music venue that first opened its doors in 1934 and accommodates up to 1,900 people. It hosts big-time music acts who often return to it as their favourite venue in Scotland, as well as bands on the rise. Many couples in Glasgow are said to have first met here over the decades.

Heading south along Kent Street, **The Barras** ❽ (http://theglasgowbarras.com; Sat–Sun 9.30am–4.30pm) originated as a street market consisting of hand-barrows hired out by the McIver family to traders too poor to have their own. In recent years, some regeneration has filtered through, with places like **Barras Art and Design** (BAaD; https://baadglasgow.com), a striking events and gig venue, much welcomed additions.

Although at first glance this busy marketplace is tatty and run-down, the area is full of life and colour, and bargain-hunters

Clothing stalls at Barras Market

The Hoops

In case you are wondering about the people bedecked in green and white stripes often seen staggering along the Gallowgate, loudly chanting songs, they are fans of Celtic Football Club, popularly known as 'The Hoops'. From the Barras, Celtic Park Stadium (www.celticfc.net) is a 15-minute walk east. Just follow the crowds on match day.

flock to it from all over the city and beyond on weekends, when the majority of shops around Barras and the Saltmarket are open. Second-hand furniture and clothes predominate. Turn left off Kent Street onto Stevenson St and you'll see St Alphonsus Church. Next door is **Randall's Antiques Market** (Sat–Sun 9am–5pm), which has a café attached.

GLASGOW GREEN

Between London Road and the River Clyde are the wide, tree-lined spaces of **Glasgow Green** ❾. Reputedly Britain's oldest public park, the Green has been common land since 1450, when King James II granted it to the people under care of Bishop William Turnbull (who was also instrumental in establishing Glasgow University). Glaswegians hold it very dear, considering it to be an immortal link between themselves and their ancestors, for whom a stroll on the Green was a favourite Sunday afternoon jaunt.

You can still see the cast iron Victorian washing poles arranged in neat rows in front of **Templeton on the Green** ❿, where women would take their washing from the wash houses (aka *steamies*) to dry. The extraordinary Templeton Carpet Factory building was designed by William Leiper as an enthusiastic copy of the Doge's Palace in Venice. Its brick and moulded terracotta edifice, complete with turrets, arched windows and mosaic-style patterns was completed in 1892. It now hosts, among other things, a business centre and **West Brewery** (www.westbeer.com; tours: Fri 6pm, Sat noon & 3pm, Sun 3pm) *bier halle* and microbrewery.

Various monuments are dotted around the lawns of Glasgow Green: **McLennan Arch** is a triumphant arch rescued from the demolished Assembly Rooms on Ingram Street, with panels featuring the Three Graces and Apollo with his lyre; the 146ft-high **Nelson Monument**; and a stern monument extolling the evils of drink and the glory of God, which was erected in the 19th century, by the Temperance movement.

THE PEOPLE'S PALACE

Glasgow Green's most conspicuous building is **The People's Palace ⑪** (www.glasgowlife.org.uk; Mon–Thu & Sat 10am–5pm, Fri & Sun 11am–5pm; free). The social history museum within houses a wonderfully haphazard evocation of the city's people since the 18th century and has long been a favourite with Glaswegians. When it opened in 1898, Lord Rosebery declared the grandiose civic project: 'A palace of pleasure and imagination around which the people may place their affections and which may give them a home on which their memory may rest'.

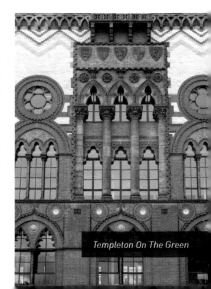

Templeton On The Green

Various themes with a particular resonance in Glasgow are explored here, including alcohol – look out for the '**Drunk's Barrow**' in which inebriated Glaswegians were carted off to jail for the night – and the bell from the notorious **Duke Street Prison**, which rang when someone was hanged on the Green.

More cheerfully, the section on the Barras recalls evenings of dancing and merriment at the nearby Barrowland Ballroom and the museum also offers ome guidance on understanding 'the Patter' – Glaswegians' idiosyncratic version of the English language. There's also a reconstruction of a 'single-end' or one-roomed house, a typical setting for the daily life of many Glaswegians through the years. For all this, though, the star exhibit is arguably Billy Connolly's pair of big banana boots.

On the top floor of the museum is a powerful series of paintings by artist and Glasgow School of Art graduate Ken Currie, who was commissioned to mark the 1987 bicentenary of the massacre of Glasgow's Calton weavers, Scotland's first trade union martyrs. His series of eight paintings adorns the splendid dome: the cycle, which traces the development of the Scottish labour movement, begins in 1787 and ends with a vision of the future. The impressive **Victorian glasshouse** at the back of the palace contains the **Winter Gardens**, a huge conservatory housing tropical palms and ferns. At the time of writing they

Banana boots

Billy Connolly's outrageous banana boots became Scottish star's trademark. Designed by Glaswegian pop artist Edmund Smith, on completion of the first boot he indicated that the second would not be identical, giving it 'designer status' by adding the famous Fyffes fruit company label. The boots made their first appearance on stage in Aberdeen in August 1975.

The Winter Gardens at
The People's Palace

were closed indefinitely,
while the funding needed
to renovate them fully
was sourced.

In front of The People's
Palace, the magnificent
red-terracotta **Doulton
Fountain** commemorates
Queen Victoria's Golden
Jubilee of 1887. Its five-
tier, 46ft (14m) -high and
70ft (21m) -wide display of
imperial pride makes it the
largest terracotta fountain
in the world and a tell-
ing insight into Glasgow's
prominent place in the British Empire. It was first unveiled at
the **Empire Exhibition** held at Kelvingrove Park in 1888 and
then moved to Glasgow Green in 1890. Walk around it to get
a closer look at extravagant figurative groups representing
Australia, Canada, India and South Africa. Seek out national
flora and fauna (Australian sheep, Canadian beaver and South
Africa's ostrich), alongside military and naval figures including
a kilted highlander, complemented by an array of gargoyles,
coats of arms, lion masks and young girls pouring water over
the figures below. Topping the whole enterprise is a statue of
Queen Victoria.

MERCHANT CITY

The grid of streets that lie immediately west of the East End is
known as **Merchant City**, an area of 18th century warehouses and

homes once bustling with cotton, tobacco and sugar traders. In the last two decades the area has been sandblasted and swabbed clean with greater enthusiasm and more municipal money than any other part of Glasgow in an attempt to bring residents back into the city centre; the resulting designer shops, stylish bars, and cafés give the area a pervasive air of sophistication.

Ingram Street, running east to west, is lined by buildings harbouring exclusive designer labels, not least the ravishing former bank that is now home to Jigsaw (No. 177). Other labels nearby include Ralph Lauren (No. 208), Mulberry (Nos. 204-7) and Hugo Boss (No. 192). If it's jewellery you're after, head to ORRO (12 Wilson Street), where you'll find unique pieces by independent designers.

TRONGATE

Running parallel to Ingram Street, two blocks to the south, is Trongate, another major shopping area and home of exciting arts developments including **Trongate 103** ⓬ (www.facebook. com/trongate103; Tues–Sat 10am–5pm, Sun noon–5pm; free), a sparkling, six-storey arts hub housing a range of workshops and galleries across various art forms, and exhibiting print-making, contemporary photography, video work and ceramics in airy, light-filled spaces.

Of the highlights, **Sharmanka Kinetic Gallery** (www.shar manka.com; show times vary) is one of Glasgow's most unusual attractions. Founded by Russian émigrés Eduard Bersudsky and Tatyana Jakovskaya, the gallery is like a mad inventor's magical workshop, with dozens of allegorical contraptions made from old wheels, levers, lights, carved wooden figures, and scrap metal which spark into life during performances. A unique art form, Sharmanka (Russian for 'barrel organ' or 'hurdy-gurdy') is at once hypnotic, playful and poignant, where mechanical sculptures, or 'kinemats', are imprisoned in a relentless routine while choreographed lighting draws the spectator from one part of the show to the next and fairground music plays in the background.

CANDLERIGGS

At the junction of Candleriggs and Bell Street, the **Glasgow Police Museum** ⓭ (www.policemuseum.org.uk; Apr–Oct Mon–Sat 10am–4.30pm & Sun noon–4.30pm, Nov–Mar Tue 10am–4.30pm & Sun noon–4.30pm; free) gives an insight into the history of Britain's first police force, as well as featuring informative exhibits on international policing. The entrance is a little tricky to find, squeezed between a bar and restaurant, and the museum is on the first floor.

The Tolbooth Steeple, Merchant City

Commemorative plaque, Ramshorn Kirk

Merchant Square contains lots of lively pubs and restaurants occupying various old buildings, although much of it lay closed for years until enthusiasts from the performing arts section of the council realised that its cobbled streets and balconied offices, which used to ring to the iron wheels of carts and the shouts of traders, would make an ideal New Orleans-style venue for the annual **Glasgow Jazz Festival**. The extensively refurbished **City Halls** (www.glasgowconcerthalls.com) is a traditional shoebox-style auditorium renowned for its acoustics. The **BBC Scottish Symphony Orchestra** is based here and the auditorium hosts performances by the Scottish Chamber Orchestra as well. Shows take place here regularly.

INGRAM STREET

Back on Ingram Street, the **Ramshorn Kirk** looms out of an unlikely grove of urban elms. The Gothic church with its square clock tower is properly known as St David's (Ramshorn) and was built in 1824 on the Ramshorn estate. Its alluring style – tall and narrow, with beautifully proportioned dimensions, soaring stained-glass windows, and substantial crypt – show all the hallmarks of Gothic Scottish Baronial Revival style. It is built in handsome blond sandstone mined from a nearby quarry at Cowcaddens, and its 120ft (36m)-high tower, towards the front of the building, houses a set of bells which have, curiously, never been rung.

The **Ramshorn Cemetery** is a verdant respite from street noise and a fascinating echo from the past. Many gravestones are so old as to be illegible, and some are still barred and spiked against the predations of grave robbers. Emile L'Angelier, arsenic victim of the infamous Madeleine Smith, is buried here, as is David Dale, philanthropic co-founder of New Lanark, and John 'Phosphorus' Anderson, the ebullient father of Strathclyde University.

Passing the delicate white spire of **Hutcheson Hall**, an early 19th century building designed by Scottish architect David Hamilton, you come to the Robert Adam-designed **Trades Hall** ⑯ (www.tradeshallglasgow.co.uk), easily distinguished by its green copper dome. Purpose-built in 1794, it still functions as the headquarters of the 14 Glasgow trade guilds. These include corporations of Bakers, Hammermen, Gardeners and Weavers, among others, although today they have limited connections to their respective trades and act more as charitably-minded associations. Their symbol – 14 arrows bound together – adorns the magnificent curving staircase that leads into the grand hall. The former civic pride and status of the guilds is still evident from the rich assortment of carvings and stained-glass windows, with a lively representation of the different trades in the silk frieze around the walls of the first-floor grand hall. Visitors are free to look around the building, and access is only restricted if there is a function.

GLASGOW CENTRAL

Glasgow Central is a perfectly compact city centre and very simple to navigate thanks to its street being laid out in a grid.

Although it holds comparatively few of the city's main sights, this neighbourhood has more than enough diversion to occupy most people for many hours. There's fine dining, great nightlife, culture in various guises, exquisite architecture, and plenty of history and shopping. Glasgow Central, Argyle Street and Queen Street train stations are all within minutes of one another on foot, as is Buchanan Bus Station and St Enoch subway station.

GEORGE SQUARE

The imposing architecture of **George Square** ⑰ reflects the confidence of Glasgow's Victorian age. At the centre of the wide-open plaza rises an 80ft column topped by a statue of Sir Walter Scott. Arranged around the great writer, at the edge of the square, are statues of assorted luminaries, ranging from Queen Victoria to Scots heroes such as James Watt and Rabbie Burns.

The florid splendour of the **City Chambers** ⑱ (Ground Floor only, Mon–Fri 8.30am–5pm), opened by Queen Victoria in 1888, occupies the entire eastern end of George Square. Built from wealth gained by colonial trade and heavy industry, it epitomizes the aspirations and optimism of late Victorian city elders. Its intricately-detailed facade includes high-minded friezes typical of the era: the four nations which comprise the United Kingdom at the feet of the enthroned queen, the British colonies, and allegorical figures representing Religion, Virtue and Knowledge.

The vaulted ceiling of the entrance hall is covered with an astonishing 1.5 million Venetian mosaic tiles. The Chambers mosaic coat of arms on the floor has four emblems – a bird, tree, bell and fish – representing legends about Glasgow's patron saint, St Mungo.

The only way to see the labyrinthine interior is to join a guided tour (Mon–Fri 10.30am and 2.30pm), which begins at the bottom of a magnificent Italian marble stairwell; the highlight of the tour (which may be restricted owing to council business) is a visit to the council chamber, richly furnished in Spanish dark mahogany and embossed leather. The Lord Provost (the Scottish equivalent of Mayor) presides over the city's affairs here. There are seats for all 79 councillors, their Deputy, and the Chief Executive, who are seated behind the mace. If you want to see the chamber in full swing, you can book a place in the public gallery to attend one of the council meetings (tel: 0141-287 4018), which are held roughly every six weeks on a Thursday.

In front of the city chambers is the lion-flanked, truncated obelisk **Cenotaph** where, since its unveiling in 1924, people from across the city and beyond have congregated to pay tribute to the fallen soldiers of World War I.

THE GALLERY OF MODERN ART

The focal point of **Royal Exchange Square** is the graceful mansion built in 1775 for tobacco lord William Cunninghame. This was the most ostentatious of the Glasgow merchants' homes and, having served as the city's Royal Exchange and Stirling Library, it now houses the **Gallery of Modern Art** ⑲ (GoMA;

Glasgow Central station

Shoppers on Buchanan Street

www.glasgowlife.org.uk; Mon–Wed & Sat 10am–5pm, Thu until 8pm, Fri & Sun 11am–5pm). The building is guarded by a statue by Baron Marocchetti of Wellington on horseback (which revellers relentlessly crown with traffic cones).

GoMA opened in 1996 to a welter of controversy about its collection. Many critics damned it for populism, stating that it failed to live up to the potential of the building. But visitors have voted with their feet, and attendance continues to exceed expectations. It is divided into four galleries and there is a café in the basement by the GoMA Library. The cavernous ground-floor space retains its columns and original classical features, lending itself to bold installations. The upper galleries use natural light wonderfully, and concentrate on group shows that often tackle challenging themes.

Free city walking tours (www.glasgowgander.com; Tue–Fri 10.30, times may vary; tip appreciated) start in front of GoMA.

BUCHANAN STREET

The wide avenue of **Buchanan Street** is the city's most prestigious shopping area. At the southern, lower end, the long pedestrian street leads north like a Victorian canyon, fronted by designer names. In the centre is the winged *Spirit of St Kentigern* statue. Buskers, from lone evangelists to full string quartets, provide daily entertainment.

On the east side is the **Argyll Arcade**, an enclosed walkway lined with jewellers' shops, which leads in a right-angle back to Argyle Street. Nearby, the **Princes Square shopping centre** is hollowed out of a sandstone building. The interior is all recherché Art Deco and ornate ironwork, filled with high-end fashion stores. It is best entered via the central escalator, past *trompe l'oeil* paintings of such luminaries as Sir Thomas Lipton, Keir Hardie, and John Logie Baird.

Turning west onto Mitchell Lane, you will find the spectacularly-converted Charles Rennie Mackintosh building, **The Lighthouse ⑳** (www.thelighthouse.co.uk; Mon–Sat 10.30am–5pm, Sun noon–5pm; free), Scotland's Centre for Design and Architecture. This was Mackintosh's first public commission, built in 1895, and housed the offices of the *Glasgow Herald* newspaper until 1980; despite glass and sandstone additions, it retains many original features, including its namesake tower.

The building's star attraction is the superb **Mackintosh Interpretation Centre**, on the third floor. It's an illuminating trawl through Mackintosh's oeuvre, with plans, photographs, models, and video displays exploring the themes behind his architecture and interiors. Elsewhere, paintings and book cover designs further demonstrate Mackintosh's outstanding versatility. There's also a varied programme of temporary exhibitions relating to architecture and design. There's a viewing platform on the sixth floor, although the best city views are from the Water Tower.

NELSON MANDELA PLACE

Passing a variety of stores including AllSaints, Hector Russell (kilts) and Apple, Buchanan Street meets **Nelson Mandela Place**, at the centre of which is **St George's Tron** , built in 1807 to accommodate the westward movement of the city. It was designed by William Stark, who was also responsible for a jail on Glasgow Green and a psychiatric hospital. The Tron has a long tradition of being at the evangelical wing of the Church of Scotland, and if you pop in today you are sure to be greeted by an enthusiastic minister.

⊙ CHARLES RENNIE MACKINTOSH

The work of the architect Charles Rennie Mackintosh (1868–1928) has come to be synonymous with the image of Glasgow. He created buildings of great beauty, idiosyncratically fusing Scots Baronial with Gothic, Art Nouveau, and modern design styles. The prevalence of his work around Glasgow has made it a pilgrimage centre for art and design students from across the world. Mackintosh's big break came in 1896, when he won the competition to design a new home for the Glasgow School of Art.

In the 1890s Glasgow went wild for tearooms, where people could play billiards and chess, read in the library, or merely chat. Over a period of twenty years Mackintosh designed articles from teaspoons to furniture and, finally, as with Mackintosh at the Willow, the structure itself. But the building that arguably displays Mackintosh at his most flamboyant was one he never saw built, the House for an Art Lover, constructed in Bellahouston Park in 1996, 95 years after the plans were submitted to a German architectural competition.

On the south side of Nelson Mandela Place is the early French Gothic extravagance of the former **Glasgow Stock Exchange** building, which brings to mind the London Law Courts and is a rather rare flight of fancy amid the solidity of its surroundings. On the north side is the former Old Athenaeum which, on opening in 1888, offered classes in science, philosophy and literature to more than 1,000 students. It now houses the Hard Rock Café.

Glasgow Stock Exchange

Opposite St George's Tron is the **VisitScotland Glasgow iCentre** (www.visitscotland.com; May–June Mon–Sat 9am–6pm, Sun 10am–4pm, July–Aug Mon–Sat 9am–7pm, Sun 10am–5pm, Sept–Apr Mon–Sat 9am–5pm, Sun 10am–4pm). It is a great place to pick up leaflets and maps, and experts can provide local and national information. They can also book transport, accommodation or tours on your behalf, locally and across Scotland. You can purchase tickets for the local sightseeing bus trips to different destinations in Scotland, as well as various attractions and events.

BUCHANAN GALLERIES

The northern end of Buchanan Street is capped by the vast **Buchanan Galleries** ㉒ shopping centre, stuffed with a raft of chain stores. It also contains **The Glasgow Royal Concert**

Hall (www.glasgowconcerthalls.com), the city's main venue for big-name touring orchestras and the home of the Royal Scottish National Orchestra. It also features major rock and R&B stars. Just below the Royal Concert Hall is a statue of Donald Dewar, Scotland's First Minister until his untimely death in 2000.

CENTRE WEST

Buchanan Street swings west onto **Sauchiehall Street**, which runs in a straight line past some unexciting shopping malls to a few of the city's most interesting sights. A few blocks either side of Sauchiehall you will find a concentration of excellent venues for the Scottish Arts including theatre, classical music and contemporary art.

The Glasgow Royal Concert Hall

One such example is Glasgow's oldest playhouse still in operation, the **Theatre Royal** ㉓ (www.glasgowtheatreroyal.org.uk) on Hope Street. Dating from 1867, this is the opulent home of the Scottish Opera and Scottish Ballet. It also plays regular host to visiting orchestras and theatre groups, including the Royal Shakespeare Company.

Across Cowcaddens Road, the **National Piping Centre** (www.thepiping centre.co.uk) prides itself on being an international centre for the promotion of the bagpipe. For the casual visitor, the single-room museum is of most interest, with a fascinating collection of instruments and related artefacts. The museum features Highland pipes from the 18th century through to the present day, as well as instruments from the European bagpipe tradition such as the Hungarian *duda*, Spanish *gaita* and Italian *zampogna* bagpipes. You can even have a go yourself on the bagpipes and a chanter (a practice pipe).

SAUCHIEHALL STREET

Charles Rennie Mackintosh fans should head for the **Mackintosh at the Willow** ㉔ (formerly The Willow Tearooms; www.mackintoshatthewillow.com), which were originally created for Kate Cranston – one of the architect's few contemporary supporters in the city – in 1903. Taking inspiration from the word *Sauchiehall*, which means 'avenue of willow', Mackintosh chose the willow leaf as a theme to unify the whole structure, from the tables to the mirrors and the ironwork. The motif is most apparent in the stylized linear panels of the bow window, which continues into the intimate dining room as it to surround the sitter, like a willow grove. These elongated forms were used to enhance the small space and demonstrate Mackintosh's superb ability to fuse function with decoration.

Rising above Sauchiehall Street to the north is one of the city centre's steepest hills, with Dalhousie and Scott streets veering up to Renfrew Street, where you'll find Charles Rennie Mackintosh's **Glasgow School of Art** ㉕ (GSofA; www.gsa. ac.uk) at number 167 – one of the most prestigious art schools in the UK. Widely considered to be the pinnacle of Mackintosh's work, the school is a characteristically angular building of warm sandstone that, due to financial constraints, had to be

constructed in two stretches (1897–99 and 1907–09). There's a clear change in the architect's style from the mock-Scottish Baronial-style east wing to the softer lines of the western half.

Tragically, in May 2014, a fire took hold in the west wing, destroying studios, archival stores and, worst of all, the library. Restoration work was ongoing when another fire broke out, in June 2018, which was so bad it even forced the O2 ABC music venue next door to close. At the time of writing the O2, and GSofA's visitor centre, shop and exhibition spaces, were all closed. Check website for

Across Scott Street from the O2 ABC stands the superb **Centre for Contemporary Arts** ❷❻ (www.cca-glasgow.com; galleries: Tue–Sat 11am–6pm, Sun noon–6pm), which has an eclectic programme, mounting six exhibitions a year. Alongside the changing visual arts exhibitions there are interactive performance-based art workshops, cinema screenings (lots of independent films, shorts, documentaries and classics) and a superb programme of musical events, ranging from improvised soundscapes, to traditional Gaelic nights, and dance-focused DJ sets. Visiting performers and artists from all over the world mean there is always something intriguing on the bill.

ST VINCENT STREET

Heading south along Pitt Street for about 300m, you will come to the **Glasgow City Free Church of Scotland** ❷❼ (www.glasgow cityfreechurch.org), the best remaining example of the work of Alexander 'Greek' Thomson (1817–75). Thomson, paradoxically, is famous for being Glasgow's 'forgotten architect', forever in the shadow of Charles Rennie Mackintosh. Like Mackintosh, he wanted to design every detail of a commission, down to the decorations on the walls. This is the only one of his three city churches still intact, and it has been added

Jessie Ware performs at King Tut's Wah Wah Hut

to the World Monument Watch's list of endangered buildings. Light from enormous windows bathes the sumptuous interior and the tower dominates Blythswood Hill.

One of Glasgow's most revered music venues, **King Tut's Wah Wah Hut** (www.kingtuts.co.uk), is just across the street at basement level. Perhaps best known as the place where Oasis were discovered, King Tut's still enjoys one of the city's best live music programmes: Liam Gallagher, Snow Patrol and The Killers have all made appearances here, along with many an up-and-comer.

Further west, down the hill a little, the needle spire of **St Columba's Gaelic Church** soars heavenwards. It originated to serve the influx of Highlanders who flocked to the city in the 18th and 19th centuries after the so-called Clearances, when landlords evicted crofters from their rented homes to make way for sheep.

CHARING CROSS

North on Elmbank Street, next to Charing Cross train station, is **The King's Theatre** 28 (tel: 0844-871 7648). This was the most fashionable Glasgow venue of the Edwardian age. Built in 1904, with a stone lion mascot above the entrance, it provides a stage for a variety of shows, catering to most ages and tastes. Expect lots of West End-style musicals and popular musical extravaganzas. Stand-up comedy shows from the likes of Stewart Lee and Frankie Boyle are also popular, plus the odd ballet production or panto thrown in for good measure.

It pays to keep this Edwardian splendour in mind on the walk north to **The Tenement House** 29 (www.nts.org.uk; Mar–Oct daily 10am–5pm, Nov–late Dec & Jan–Feb Sat–Mon 11am–4pm). It lies at the end of the leafy walkway at 145 Buccleuch Street and its glimpse into tenement life is fascinating. For 50 years it was the home of Agnes Toward, who changed nothing in her 'wally close' (tiled common stairway).

On the ground floor, there's an display on the development of the humble tenement block as the bedrock of urban Scottish housing, with a poignant display of relics – ration books, letters, bills, holiday snaps and so forth – from Agnes's life. The ground floor is also home

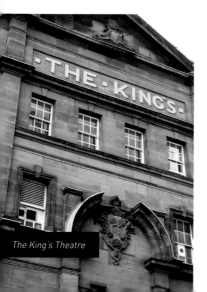

The King's Theatre

to a visitor centre with an exhibition space and a shop, while the opposite ground-floor flat hosts temporary exhibitions about life in old Glasgow.

Upstairs, you have to ring the doorbell to enter the flat, whose four rooms give every impression of still being inhabited; the cluttered kitchen features a superb cast-iron range, cupboards crammed with utensils (one has a full jar of jam from 1929), and a box-bed, known colloquially as a 'hurley', which would sleep up to five children. Elsewhere, there are framed religious tracts, a sewing machine, and a walnut- and rose-wood piano, which it is believed both Agnes and her mother played.

To delve deeper into the history of life in Glasgow, head to the splendidly-domed **Mitchell Library** ㉚ (www.glasgowlife. org.uk; Mon–Thu 9am–8pm, Fri–Sat until 5pm), adorned with a statue of Minerva rising above the traffic below. It is now the biggest public reference library in Europe, and its comprehensive Glasgow Room is a boon and a blessing to those with an interest in the city. It has fabulous, free resources for those looking to research family history or anyone just curious about the city's past.

THE WEST END

The urbane **West End** seems a world away from Glasgow's industrial image. In the 1800s the city's wealthy merchants established huge estates away from the soot and grime of city life, and in 1870 the ancient university was moved from its cramped home near the cathedral to a spacious new site overlooking the River Kelvin. Elegant housing swiftly followed: the **Kelvingrove Art Gallery and Museum** was built to house the 1888 International Exhibition, and, in 1896, the **Glasgow District Subway** started its shuffle from here to the city centre.

The hub of life in this part of Glasgow is **Byres Road**, running between Great Western Road and Dumbarton Road past Hillhead Subway station. Shops, restaurants, cafés, pubs and hordes of people, including thousands of students, lend a buzz to the area. Glowing red-sandstone tenements and graceful terraces provide a suitably stylish backdrop to this cosmopolitan district.

KELVINGROVE

Approaching from the city centre, a good starting point is the splendid oval of **Park Circus**, with its air of Victorian elegance. The grand curving terraces rising to a bluff above the River Kelvin)were designed as private housing for the emergent middle classes by Charles Wilson (1810–63) and can justly be regarded as his masterpiece. The terraces lead to **Kelvingrove Park** ③ (www.kelvingrovepark.com), site of three great

⊙ GLASGOW'S GREEN SPACES

The Victorians viewed public parks as the lungs of their smoky cities, allowing their workers the physically and morally beneficial effects of clean air and uplifting scenery. Glasgow Green was the only public space in the city until 1846, when a grand plan was proposed by the city council to create three huge sculpted parklands – Kelvingrove in the west, Alexandra Park in the east and Queen's Park in the south – under the hand of designer Sir Joseph Paxton, of Crystal Palace fame. The city now boasts more than 70 parks, and although the recreational facilities reflect Victorian tastes – boating ponds, playgrounds, putting and bowling – the work of the inventive and industrious Parks Department has given each its own character.

International Exhibitions, in 1888, 1901 and 1911, which proudly proclaimed Glasgow's contribution to the British Empire. The entrance to Kelvingrove Park is guarded by a spectacular statue of Field Marshal Earl Roberts of Kandahar (1832–1914) surrounded by the bas-relief trappings of his Indian campaigns.

Kelvingrove Park

The park itself is a fine example of an ornamental pleasure garden, with winding paths and wide boulevards. As you descend into the park, the main thoroughfare and bridge are marked by a memorial to the officers and men of the Highland Light Infantry who fell in the 'South African War' or Boer War (1899–1902). Turning south here, the path leads through dappled shade to the extravagance of the **Stewart Memorial Fountain**, a tribute to the Lord Provost who, in 1855, finally managed to secure a supply of pure water to the city from Loch Katrine in the Trossachs.

Turning west past the skateboard park and the duck ponds, the tour emerges onto the Kelvin Walkway and a bridge cornered by four groups of bronzes representing peace and war, commerce and industry, shipping and navigation, and prosperity and progress.

Founded on donations from the city's Victorian industrialists and opened at an international fair held in 1901, the huge, red

The Kelvin Walkway

There are lots of fabulous opportunities for cycling and walking in and around Kelvingrove Park and the Botanic Gardens. One less well-known route follows the Kelvin Walkway and links up with the Forth and Clyde Canal towpath at the Kelvin Aqueduct – an impressive feat of 18th-century engineering and architecture, which was once the largest functioning aqueduct in Europe.

sandstone fantasy castle of **Kelvingrove Art Gallery and Museum** ㉜ (www.glasgowlife.org.uk; Mon–Thu & Sat 10am–5pm, Fri & Sun 11am–5pm; free) is a brash statement of Glasgow's 19th century self-confidence. Holding one of the finest civic collections in Europe, it is intricate both in its riotous exterior and superb interiors, where a galleried main hall runs the length of the building, giving way to attractive upper balconies and small, interlinked display galleries. There are recitals on the giant Lewis pipe organ in the Centre Hall at 1pm (3pm on Sundays).

The displays are organized under two principal headings: Life, in the western half of the building, encompassing archaeology, local history and stuffed animals, and Expression, in the eastern half, which houses much of the superb art collection. There's much to absorb, and a repeat visit may be in order.

Inevitably though, it's the paintings that draw the biggest crowds, the most famous of which is Salvador Dalí's radically foreshortened *Christ of St John of the Cross*, located on the South Balcony. The focus of huge controversy when it was purchased by the city in 1952, for what was regarded as the vast sum of £8,200, it has become an icon of the collection and essential viewing on any visit. Other favourites include Rembrandt's calm *A Man in Armour*, Van Gogh's *The Blute-Fin*

Windmill and his *Portrait of Alexander Reid* (of Glasgow art dealer with whom he once briefly shared a flat in Paris), and a very strong French presence, with at least one painting apiece by Monet, Gauguin, Pissarro, Cézanne and Renoir.

You can also acquaint yourself with significant Scottish art including works by the Glasgow Boys and the Scottish Colourists, the latter heavily influenced by the French school, as demonstrated in wildly colourful pieces like *Landscape* and *Laggan Farm Buildings near Dalbeattie* by Samuel Peploe. There's also a special section of paintings, furniture and murals devoted to Charles Rennie Mackintosh and the 'Glasgow Style' that he and his contemporaries inspired.

In all, the collection includes more than 8,000 objects over three floors and many interactive displays. Within the walls of this cultural treasure trove, visitors to the West Wing will find a World War II Spitfire hanging from the ceiling and Sir Roger, a stuffed elephant which was once a resident of the Glasgow Zoo.

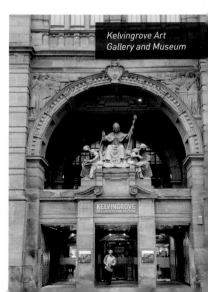

Kelvingrove Art Gallery and Museum

Leaving from the west end of the art gallery, past the 'machine-gun Tommy' war memorial, cross the street to the **Kelvin Hall** (http://kelvinhall.org.uk), which for many years was Glasgow's foremost exhibition centre. A £60 million redevelopment saw it reopen in 2016 with state-of-the-art facilities including Scotland's Moving Image Archive, temporary exhibitions, a café, a gym and tours of the Glasgow Museums' stores.

THE UNIVERSITY OF GLASGOW

Dominating the West End skyline, the turreted tower of the **University of Glasgow** (www.gla.ac.uk), designed by Sir George Gilbert Scott in the mid-19th century, overlooks the

---

⊘ THE GLASGOW BOYS AND THE COLOURISTS

In the 1870s a group of eminent Glasgow-based painters, such as James Guthrie, John Lavery, George Henry, E. A. Hornel and Joseph Crawhall, became known as the Glasgow Boys. They came from different backgrounds, but all rejected the oppressively sentimental eighteenth-century renditions of Scottish history peopled by "poor but happy" families. Sharing a passion for realism and naturalism, and taking inspiration from the *plein-air* painting of the Impressionists, they began to experiment with colour. The content of their work often embraced these principles to depict peasant life and work.

The Glasgow Boys school did not outlast World War I, but they inspired the next generation of Edinburgh painters, who became known as the Scottish Colourists. Samuel John Peploe, John Duncan Fergusson, George Leslie Hunter and Francis Cadell shared an understanding that the manipulation of colour was the heart and soul of a good painting. The influence of Post-Impressionists such as Matisse and Cézanne is obvious in the work of all four, with their seascapes, society portraits and still-lives bursting with fluidity, unconventionality and the manipulation of colour and shape.

glades edging the River Kelvin; the university itself was founded in 1451, which ranks it as the fourth oldest in the English-speaking world (after St Andrew's, Oxford and Cambridge), and was originally located near the cathedral on High Street. In 1870 it moved to its current site.

The University of Glasgow

Access to the main buildings and museums is from University Avenue, running east from Byres Road. In the dark neo-Gothic pile under the tower you'll find the **University Visitor Centre & Shop** (Mon–Sat 9.30am–5pm, Sun 11am–4pm). Student-led tours (tel: 0141-330 5360; http://src.glasgow.ac.uk/tours; Apr–Oct 11am & 2pm, Nov–Mar 2pm) of the campus begin here. Although no buildings are entered, the tour focuses on the university's history, taking in the grounds, statues, tombstones and the like.

THE HUNTERIANS

A staircase by the Visitor Centre leads to sunlit quadrangles and contrastingly moody cloisters. Here also is the lusciously ornate Bute Hall and the **Hunterian Museum** ㉝ (www.gla.ac.uk/hunterian; Tue–Sat 10am–5pm, Sun 11am–4pm; free), which displays the death mask of founder and former student, William Hunter. Its splendid galleries house material of great antiquity, including dinosaurs' eggs and a superb ceremonial

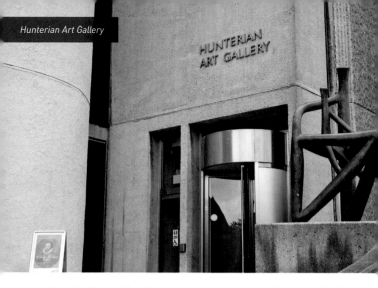

Maori knife inlaid with shark's teeth from Captain Cook's third voyage. Upstairs is Lord Kelvin's exhaustive collection of scientific instruments, one of the most notable objects being a gas discharge tube presented to him by Nikola Tesla, the leading physicist of the time.

The Hunterian's most outstanding exhibit, however, is entitled *The Antonine Wall: Rome's Final Frontier*; a shorter counterpart to Hadrian's Wall further south, this sophisticated structure was built around 142 AD and ran from Clyde to the Firth of Forth. On display are sixteen distance slabs (it's thought that there were nineteen), carved stones that document the work of the legions, alongside funerary monuments, domestic items and sculptural stones, a quite unique ensemble from the Roman Empire.

The round building directly across from the university gatehouse is the **McMillan Reading Room**, to the east of which lies

Wellington Church. The grand classical structure was influenced by the Madeleine in Paris, with 10 massive fluted pillars supporting its portico. There is a small café in the crypt.

To the west of the McMillan Reading Room lies the **Hunterian Art Gallery** ❸❹ (www.gla.ac.uk/hunterian; Tue–Sat 10am–5pm, Sun 11am–4pm; free). It houses the internationally famous collection by James Abbott McNeill Whistler; only the Smithsonian has a larger collection. Whistler's portraits of women give his subjects a resolute strength in addition to their occasionally winsome qualities: look out especially for the trio of full-length portraits, *Harmony of Flesh Colour*; *Black, Pink and Gold: The Tulip* and *Red and Black: The Fan*, as well as his dreamy night-time visions of the Thames. Whistler's most important piece, however, is *The Rich and Poor Peacock*, a decorative mural designed for Frederick Leyland's Peacock Room in London, which supposedly symbolized the fractious relationship between artist and client.

With works by Rembrandt, Pissarro and Rodin, plus works by the Glasgow Boys and the Scottish Colourists, the museum has put together an impressive collection of contemporary art. Scottish artists are well represented, including works by Henry (keep an eye out for the striking The Hedge Cutter), Hornel and Paterson, whose lovely *Morning in Glencairn* is suggestive of southern France but is in fact south of Glasgow near Dumfries.

The more recently acquired works have a naturalistic, scientific element that complements the overall collection. The fascinating work of Mark Dion is inspired by the powerful historic role of great museum collections such as the Hunterian's. Other contemporary art highlights worth seeking out are Christine Borland's delicate skulls entitled *Family Conversation Piece: Head of Father* (1998), and Matt Collishaw's strutting peacock, which accompanies the works of Whistler.

A side gallery off the Hunterian leads to the **Mackintosh House** (www.gla.ac.uk/hunterian; Tue–Sat 10am–5pm, Sun 11am–4pm), an assemblage of the interior of the now-demolished Glasgow home of Margaret MacDonald and Charles Rennie Mackintosh. The elegant interior contains more than sixty pieces of Mackintosh furniture on three floors, many featuring his signature leaf and rose motifs. The first room is the dining room, complete with three-dimensional fireplace and a half a dozen chairs considered so futuristic that they have been used in episodes of *Babylon 5* and *Dr Who*. The studio drawing room – a startlingly modern design for that period – contains Mackintosh's ebony writing desk, while the standout items in the white-painted oak bedroom are a pair of stunning dove wardrobes and a slimming mirror. There are also plenty of his wife's possessions.

BYRES ROAD AND AROUND

Abandoning academia for more hedonistic pleasures, **Byres Road**, at the junction with University Avenue, presents itself as the students' playground. Named after a small *clachan*, or village, which once stood there called Byres of Partick, it is a cosmopolitan mix of restaurants, bars and cafés, and comfortingly solid tenement architecture. One of the key places to grab a drink and some 'scran' (food) is on the alley called **Ashton Lane**. There's Irish, Scottish, Indian, Belgian and French-style dining, as well as the **Grosvenor Cinema**. Ruthven Lane, on the opposite side of Byres Road, has antiquarian bookstores and vintage and designer clothes.

Going north up Byres Road, past Hillhead Underground, turn right onto Great George Street and then left onto **Cresswell Lane** for De Courcy's Arcade, a warren of stalls selling accessories, jewellery, crafts and retro design. At the northern end, turn left and then right again onto Byres Road to the junction with Great Western Road. On the right is the pyramid spire of the former Kelvinside Parish Church, which has been converted into the excellent **Òran Mór** ㉟ (meaning 'great melody of life' or 'big song'; www.oran-mor.co.uk) live music centre, restaurant and bar. Pop in to view the cavernous auditorium and its wonderful murals by artist and novelist Alasdair Gray.

GLASGOW BOTANIC GARDENS

Directly opposite are the **Glasgow Botanic Gardens** ㊱ (www.glasgowbotanicgardens.com; Gardens: daily 7am–dusk, Glasshouses: 10am–6pm, winter until 4.15pm; Garden Tearooms: 10am–6pm, winter until 4pm; free), a pleasant recreation space with a herb garden, vegetable garden, and some

Ashton Lane, lined with pubs and restaurants

Glasgow Botanic Gardens

dramatic greenhouses nurturing tropical plants. The delicate dome of the **Kibble Palace** was brought here from the Clyde coast home of John Kibble in 1873. An impressive structure, covering 23,000 sq ft (2,137 sq m), it now houses the magnificent National Collection of Ferns with samples from around the world. Nearby, the Main Range Glasshouse is home to lurid flowers and plants luxuriating in the humidity, including orchids, cacti, palms and tropical fruit; the annual Orchid Fair is held in mid-May.

There are some beautifully remote paths in the gardens that weave along the wooded banks of the River Kelvin, linking up with the walkway that runs alongside the river all the way down to Dumbarton Road, near its confluence with the Clyde; en-route you'll find a rose garden and a children's garden and, beyond here, the arboretum, replete with birch, fir and pine trees.

CLYDESIDE

'The **Clyde** made Glasgow and Glasgow made the Clyde' runs an old saw, full of sentimentality for the days when the river was the world's premier shipbuilding centre, and when its industry made Glasgow the second city of the British Empire. Despite the hardships that heavy industry brought,

Glaswegians would follow the progress of the skeleton ships under construction in the riverside yards, cheering them on their way down the Clyde as they were launched.

RIVERSIDE

If you follow the Kelvin River to its confluence with the Clyde, it is clear that this shipbuilding heritage has not been forgotten, with the masts of the Tall Ship *Glenlee* reflected in the mirrored facade of the superb **Riverside Museum** ❸❼ (www.glasgowlife.org.uk; Mon–Thu & Sat 10am–5pm, Fri & Sun 11am–5pm; free). This striking multi-million-pound museum, designed by the late Zaha Hadid, opened in 2011 and its severe, undulating

⊙ THE REJUVENATION OF THE CLYDE

The last of the great liners to be built on Clydeside was the *QE2* in 1967, yet such events are hard to visualize today, with the banks of the river all but devoid of any industry. For much of the 20th century the closures and demolitions of the docks, the rusting metal cranes and crumbling factories, were symptomatic of a city in decline; the detritus of Victorian Britain rotting on the banks, where the component parts of a mighty empire were once manufactured.

Today, BAE Systems' shipyard is one of the few that remains, its survival only guaranteed from one contract to the next. But the days of derelict warehouses, crumbling docks and empty wastelands marring the river's flanks are also coming to an end. The massive Clyde Waterfront Regeneration project has attracted £5-6 billion in public and private investment, and a forest of cranes on the skyline suggestion there's more regeneration to come.

roof serves as a reminder that Glasgow has an indelible and often uncomfortable relationship with the water. The lofty windows at either end act as a conduit between the river and the city, as though reuniting them.

Within, more than 3,000 objects trace the history of transport, most of them relating to Scotland, from a velodrome of bicycles suspended from the ceiling to a wall of classic cars and motorbikes spanning the decades. Most popular, particularly with children, are the old trams, bus and subway carriage – climb aboard to get a real sense of travel in days gone by. Look out for the No. 1088, which boasts a beautiful, upholstered leather interior, brass fittings and stained-glass windows. Though for sheer spectacle, nothing comes close to the formidable South African Class 15F locomotive, which

Classic vehicles at the Riverside Museum

is testament to the engineering prowess of the North British Locomotive Company in Glasgow. Continuing the nostalgic theme, there are two areas recreating streetscapes from the 1890s to the 1960s with replicas of specialist shops and pubs.

On the museum's riverside flank is **The Tall Ship** *Glenlee* (www.thetallship.com; daily Mar–Oct 10am–5pm, Nov–Feb 10am–4pm; free). The restored *Glenlee*, a Clyde-built three-masted barque, sailed the globe from the 1890s to the 1920s – journeying as far afield as Argentina, Australia and Japan – before becoming a naval training ship. The four decks can now be explored to find out what life was like on board. Visit the crews' cabins, galley, hospital and map room. There is also a good café here. Close to The Tall Ship, **Seaforce** (www.seaforce.co.uk) runs exciting powerboat rides along the Clyde, weather permitting.

The footpath heading east from the Riverside Museum passes a rather forlorn looking brownfield site, although at the other end **The Clydeside Distillery** ❸❽ (www.theclydeside. com; tours hourly from 10am–4pm) has transformed the old Pumphouse, with its copper pot stills gazing out over the Clyde through a glass-fronted edifice. This is the first dedicated single-malt whisky distillery in Glasgow for over a century.

SEC COMPLEX

The futuristic buildings ahead make up the SEC Complex. Unless you're attending a conference or a concert at the **SEC Centre** (www.sec.co.uk) or the neighbouring **SEC Armadillo** (tel: 0141-248 3000) you're unlikely to go inside either of these two colossal buildings. But their architectural splendour makes them must-sees and they have become symbolic of the whole regeneration of Glasgow from the 1980s onwards. The architect Sir Norman Foster took inspiration from this former ship-building area, designing an exterior intended to emulate ships' hulls. The newest building of the trio is the **SSE Hydro** ❸❾ (www.thessehydro.com), which welcomes the biggest names in music and comedy to its stage most nights of the week.

The final unusual structure here is the hulking **Finnieston Crane**. This huge cantilever crane was in use for more than 50 years as a means of lifting heavy machinery, but it became redundant as industry died out in the city in the 1990s. It now stands as a dramatic tribute to the great industrial heritage of Glasgow.

PACIFIC QUAY

Taking the Millennium Bridge pedestrian crossing over to the south side of the Clyde, it is possible to see the **Clyde Arc Bridge**, also known as Squinty Bridge, on your left. This is another great symbol of modern Glasgow and is especially attractive when lit up at dusk.

The south bank of the river is dominated by three space-age constructions which make up the **Glasgow Science Centre** ❹⓿ (www.glasgowsciencecentre.org; Apr–Oct daily 10am–5pm, Nov–Mar Wed–Fri 10am–3pm, Sat–Sun 10am–5pm), the largest of which is the curvaceous, wedge-shaped **Science Mall**. Inside are four floors of interactive exhibits ranging from lift-your-own-weight pulleys to high-tech thermograms.

The centre covers almost every aspect of science, from simple optical illusions to cutting-edge computer technology, including a section on moral and environmental issues. Within the mall, an impressive planetarium and 3D virtual science theatre put on shows throughout the day. Alongside the Science Mall is the bulbous **IMAX theatre** (www.cineworld.co.uk), which screens the latest blockbusters.

Glasgow Science Centre

Also on the site of the Glasgow Science Centre is the 417ft-high (127m) **Glasgow Tower**, the tallest freestanding structure in Scotland, built with an aerofoil-like construction to allow it to rotate and face into the prevailing wind. Glass lifts ascend to the viewing cabin, which offers terrific panoramic views of central Glasgow.

The two steamships moored at Pacific Quay were built along the Clyde and have each plied the waters for many decades. The **Waverley** (www.waverleyexcursions.co.uk), the world's last seagoing passenger-carrying paddle steamer, spent the summers cruising to various ports on the Firth of Clyde and the Ayrshire until boiler issues forced it to be withdrawn from service in 2019. There are hopes to make it seaworthy once more. She's an elegant vessel to look at, especially when in operation. Moored nearby, the **TS *Queen Mary*** (https://tsqueenmary.org. uk) is the latest returnee to the Clyde, having been towed up from its previous moorings in London. It was undergoing extensive refurbishment at the time of writing, and plans were afoot to send her to the dry dock. Check the website for updates.

SOUTHSIDE

The section of Glasgow south of the Clyde is generally described as the **Southside**, though within this area there are a number of districts with recognizable names, including the notoriously deprived Gorbals and Govan. This region is often overlooked by visitors, but there are some real gems that reward the effort, especially towards the more salubrious suburbs. If you don't have the use of a bike, a car would be the best means of transport, since it is not easy to travel between most sights on foot.

The wonderfully designed **Scotland Street School Museum** ❹ (www.glasgowlife.org.uk; Tue–Thu and Sat 10am–5pm, Fri and Sun 11am–5pm; free) is another of the city's Mackintosh treasures, and the one to head for if time is limited. This was Mackintosh's second commission for the School Board and the last individual building he designed in Glasgow. The school opened in 1906, before closing in 1979. The most immediately striking elements are the twin towers (one of Mackintosh's

Ibrox Stadium

When it comes to football, the blue half of Glasgow can be found in and around the Ibrox Stadium (https://rangers.co.uk) the home of Rangers F.C. 'The Gers' as they're known, have a devout following, who can often be seen wearing the badge even when it isn't match day. Ibrox SPT subway station provides easy access.

favoured design features), one an entrance for boys, the other for girls. There are reconstructed class-rooms from the Victorian era, World War II, and the 50s and 60s. One room is given over to exhibiting Mackintosh's designs, while another fondly recalls the school's history, with books, photos, and a rather grand roll-top desk belonging to William Davidson, the first head-master. Even more fasci-

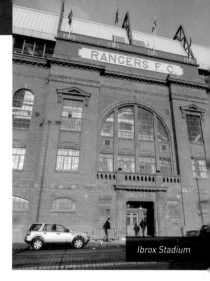

Ibrox Stadium

nating are the former pupils' recollections of their school days.

BELLAHOUSTON PARK

Tucked just inside Bellahouston Park is Mackintosh's **House for an Art Lover** ⑫ (www.houseforanartlover.co.uk; times vary owing to private events). Designed in 1901 for a German competition, it wasn't until 1987 that civil engineer Graham Roxburgh conceived the idea of building the house. It eventually opened in 1996; few original drawings for the house remained, so its design was largely based on other Mackintosh buildings. Nevertheless, it is still quintessential Mackintosh.

The house is entered via the Main Hall, a deliberately grand space with massive windows designed for large parties. Intended for women to retire to after dinner, everything in the delicate Oval Room, as well as the room itself, is oval. Next door, the dazzling white Music Room has bow windows opening

Pollok Country Park

out to a large balcony. Designed to symbolize a forest glade, features here include floor-to-ceiling pillars, teardrop leaves, clusters of lanterns, and rose stencils above the hearth – the room's most theatrical piece, though, is a wonderfully-encased piano. In complete contrast, the Dining Room is decorated with stained wood, enhanced by beautiful gesso tiles.

POLLOK COUNTRY PARK

The grandly-sculpted grounds of **Pollok Country Park** ㊸ were given to the city in 1966 by Mrs Anne Maxwell Macdonald. Thanks to her generosity, visitors can enjoy the 361-acre (146-hectare) park's Highland cattle, horses, art collection, and woodland walks in what is considered to be one of the finest, and most overlooked, parks in Europe.

In the middle sits the grandiose **Pollok House** ㊹ (www.nts. org.uk; daily 10am–5pm), a masterful William Adam construction dating from 1752. Appropriately, the house is under the management of the National Trust for Scotland, as it was in the upstairs smoking room in 1931 that the then-owner, Sir John Stirling Maxwell, held the first meetings with the Eighth Duke of Atholl and Lord Colquhoun of Luss that led to the formation of the NTS. Paintings within include Spanish masterpieces – among them two El Greco portraits and works by Murillo and

Goya – in the morning room and some splendid Dutch hunting scenes in the dining room. Sir John's own worthy, but noticeably amateur, efforts line the upstairs corridors. Free tours of the house are available from the front desk, or you can wander around at your own pace.

Heading towards the northeast leads to the internationally famous **Burrell Collection** (www.glasgowlife.org.uk; consult website for reopening updates), home to numerous priceless artworks. At the time of writing, The Burrell Collection was undergoing a vast overhaul having secured a £60-million grant to ensure that 90 per cent of the collection could be put on show. It is scheduled to reopen in Spring 2021.

The collection is eclectic and idiosyncratic, with more than 9,000 objects from Egypt, Greece, the Middle East and South and East Asia, plus tapestries and stained glass from medieval Europe. Especially notable are the Degas collection, Rodin's *Thinker* (one of 14 casts made from the original) and the *Warwick Vase*, an 8-ton marble that dominates the courtyard. During closure parts of the collection are on display at Kelvingrove Art Gallery.

OTHER NOTABLE PARKS

Located in the extensive **Linn Park** is the finest domestic design by rediscovered Glasgow architect Alexander "Greek" Thomson. **Holmwood House** 45 (www.nts.org.uk; Mar–late Apr & early Aug–late Oct Fri–Mon noon–5pm, late Apr–early Aug Sat & Sun noon–5pm) shows off Thomson's bold classical concepts, with exterior pillars on two levels and a raised main door, as well as his detailed and highly imaginative interiors. On the upper floor is the drawing room with a starlit night painting on the ceiling, which contrasts with a black marble fireplace and sunburst decorations in the parlour immediately beneath on the ground level. Across the corridor, the dining room has a frieze of scenes from the *Iliad*, along with a skylight at the back of the room, which was designed to allow the gods to peer down on the feasts being consumed inside.

Another expanse of land generously donated to the city, this time by Archibald. Cameron Corbett, 1st Baron Rowallan, in 1906, is **Rouken Glen Park** ㊻. A thriving range of commercial concerns, including an attractive garden centre, art gallery, and a signposted walkabout trail, has been added to the original attractions like the waterfall tumbling into a mossy glen, a walled garden, golf course, and generous parkland.

Although built in the reign of Victoria, and laid out by Sir Joseph Paxton of Crystal Palace fame, **Queen's Park** ㊼ was named for Mary, Queen of Scots, whose armies lost the Battle of Langside nearby, in 1568. The 148-acre (60-hectare) park occupies a commanding site, which was considerably enlarged in 1894 by the enclosure of the grounds of Camp Hill, which has been occupied since prehistoric times. There is also a pond teeming with birdlife, including tufted ducks, moorhens, mallards, little grebe, coots and mute swans.

HAMPDEN PARK

Just east of Queen's Park, the floodlights and

Rouken Glen Park

giant stands of Scotland's national football stadium, **Hampden Park** ❽ (www. hampdenpark.co.uk), loom over the surrounding suburban tenements. Home of Queen's Park Football Club, the fact that it's the venue for Scotland's international fixtures and major cup finals makes it a place of pilgrimage for the country's football fans.

Queen's Park

Queen's Park rises to an impressive summit, with panoramic views as far as Ben Lomond in the north and Lanark in the south. Near the main pathway is an oak tree planted by Belgian refugees after World War I and a beech tree planted in 1965 to commemorate the 20th anniversary of the founding of the United Nations.

The engaging **Scottish Football Museum** (https://scottishfootballmuseum.org.uk; Mon–Sat 10am–5pm, Sun 11am–5pm; times liable to change on event days) has extensive collections of memorabilia, video clips and displays. The Hall of Fame honours the likes of Denis Law, Jimmy Johnstone and Kenny Dalglish. Regular guided stadium tours offer the chance to see the changing rooms and warm-up areas before climbing the stairs for the obligatory lifting of the cup.

EXCURSIONS

Accessible on a day-trip from Glasgow are some of Scotland's most enthralling natural backdrops, popular Victorian era getaways, and sites of historic significance such as castles, stately homes, old factories, and national parks.

THE TROSSACHS

Often described as the Highlands in miniature, **Loch Lomond and the Trossachs National Park** ❾ (www.loch

lomond-trossachs.org) boasts a magnificent diversity of scenery, with distinctive peaks, silvery lochs and mysterious, forest-covered slopes. The area covers over seven hundred square miles of scenic territory. The centrepiece is undoubtedly **Loch Lomond**, and the most popular gateway is **Balloch**, the town at the loch's southern tip, where the VisitScotland tourist information centre (www.visitscotland.com) is located. Outdoors enthusiasts come to the Trossachs in droves for hiking, tours, mountain-bike excursions, horse riding, fishing and boat trips on the lochs.

Some of the best hill-walking within easy reach of Glasgow can be found in **Glen Luss**. A series of Corbetts (Scottish hills ranging between 2,500ft/762m and 3,000ft/914m) afford spectacular views to the Clyde estuary and the western islands. If you want to 'bag a Munro', which are Scotland's highest peaks over 3,000ft, then the 3,707ft (1,130m) -high **Ben Lui** (13 miles/21km, about 7 hours) is a must-climb. **Ben Lomond** (3,196ft/974m) and **Beinn Ime** (3,317ft/1,011m) also offer excellent hiking. The weather in the mountains can change quickly, so always carry a map and provisions, and dress warmly.

> ### West Highland Way
>
> The West Highland Way, a 96-mile (154km) walk from Milngavie to Fort William, starts in Glasgow's Douglas Street. The route follows ancient tracks, drove roads, military roads and disused railway lines. The first 5-mile (8km) stage to Carbeth involves 500ft (148m) of ascent, a tame preamble to the Devil's Staircase. See www.westhighlandway.org.

THE CLYDE VALLEY

When Glaswegians sing praise of the river that gave their city meaning, they think of the clatter of ship-yards and the sway of giant cranes. But further down the valley is an altogether different river, which wanders through gentle hills and waters the fertile orchards and fruit farms on its banks.

Chatelherault Country Park ⑩ (tel: 01698-426 213; visitor centre: daily 10am–5pm; West Lodge: Sun–Thu 10am–4.30pm) makes up nearly 500 acres (200 hectares) of the Avon Gorge, which runs along the River Avon, a tributary of the River Clyde. There

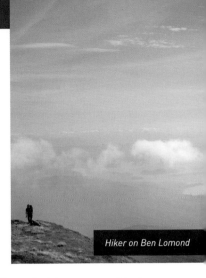

Hiker on Ben Lomond

are miles of riverside walks and picturesque sights here, including the dramatic Duke's Bridge, the medieval mystery of Cadzow Castle and rolling parkland featuring white cattle, whose lineage dates back to Roman times.

Dating back to around 1530, **Craignethan Castle** ⑪ (tel: 01555-860 364; Apr–Sept daily 9.30am–5pm), is a bulky, sombre keep. This rambling ruin was one of the last great family tower fortresses, and from it the Hamilton family played a pivotal role in Scottish politics, including supporting Mary, Queen of Scots, whom they sheltered here after her abdication in 1567.

One of the most remarkable episodes in Scotland's industrial history, as well as one of its most adventurous heritage restoration projects, is **New Lanark** ⑫ (www.newlanark.org; Apr–Oct 10am–5pm, Nov–Mar 10am–4pm). Seeming like little more than a group of stone-built warehouses, it was here that David Dale, one of Scotland's leading industrialists and philanthropists, and his son-in-law Robert Owen conducted a social experiment that was to have lasting repercussions for the bitterly oppressed working classes. In around 1799, they founded the mill village of New Lanark, which created decent housing and offered reasonable wages, education and health-care, and proved their theory that contented workers were productive workers.

The village, now a Unesco World Heritage Site, has been restored as a living community complete with hotel and shops; the old millworkers' tenement houses are now highly desirable properties. In the Visitor Centre, various audiovisual displays show life in the mill past, present and future. Along the river itself, a sylvan walk leads to the **Falls of Clyde**, where the Scottish Wildlife Trust organises badger watches, and the keen-eyed may spot kingfishers, owls and, as night descends, pipistrelle bats.

ISLANDS OF THE CLYDE

The **Firth of Clyde** filters out of Glasgow to the west and then the south, towards the Irish Sea. A number of islands make for excellent day trips from the city.

Bute

Thanks to its mild climate and its combined train/ferry link between Glasgow and Wemyss Bay, **Bute ⑤** has been a popular holiday and convalescence spot for Clydesiders for over a century. In its heyday in the 1880s, thirty steamers a day would call in at the island's capital, **Rothesay**. This handsome Victorian resort is set in a wide, sweeping bay, backed by green hills, with a classic palm-tree promenade and 1930s pagoda-style Art Deco pavilion (due to reopen as a music venue in

Craignethan Castle

2020). Incongruously located amid the town's backstreets stand the militarily useless, but architecturally impressive, moated ruins of the 12th century **Rothesay Castle** (www.his toricenvironment.scot; Apr–Sept daily 9.30am–5pm, Oct–Mar Sat–Wed 10am–4pm).

The most compelling reason to visit Bute, however, is the chance to amble around **Mount Stuart** (www.mountstuart. com; house and grounds late Mar–Oct daily 10am–4pm), one of Scotland's most singular aristocratic piles and the ancestral seat of the marquesses of Bute, designed by Robert Rowand Anderson. The *pièce de resistance* here is the columned Marble Hall, its vaulted ceiling and twelve stained-glass windows adorned with the signs of the zodiac, reflecting the 3rd marquess's taste for mysticism. He was equally fond of animal and plant imagery; hence you'll find birds feeding on berries in the dining-room frieze and monkeys reading (and tearing up) books and scrolls in the library. After all the heavy furnishings, there's aesthetic relief in the vast Marble Chapel, built entirely out of dazzling white Carrara marble, with a magnificent Cosmati floor pattern. Upstairs, the highlight is the Horoscope Room, so named after the fine astrological ceiling. Be sure to seek out the wall panels carved with occasionally amusing friezes, such as a frog playing a lute.

Arran

Shaped like a kidney bean and occupying centre stage in the Firth of Clyde, **Arran** ⁵⁴ is often dubbed 'Scotland in miniature'. The north is mountainous and sparsely populated, while the lush southern half enjoys a much milder climate.

Rothesay Castle

There are two big crowd-pullers on Arran: geology and golf. The former has fascinated rock-obsessed students since Sir James Hutton came here in the late 18th century to confirm his theories of uniformitarianism. A hundred years later, Sir Archibald Geikie's investigations were a landmark in the study of Arran's geology, and the island remains a popular destination for university and school field trips. As for golf, Arran boasts seven courses.

The resort of **Brodick** (from the Norse *breidr vik*, 'broad bay') hosts the **Arran Heritage Museum** (www.arranmuseum.co.uk; late Mar–late Oct daily 10.30am–4pm). Housed in a white-washed 18th century crofter's farm, it contains an old 'smiddy' (blacksmith's workshop) and a twee Victorian cottage with box-bed and range. In the old stables, an exhibition considers the island's intriguing geological and archaeological heritage. There is also an incredibly well-preserved early Bronze Age cist grave, complete with intact food vessel.

Further north of town lies the former seat of the duke of Hamilton, **Brodick Castle** (www.nts.org.uk; Apr–late Dec 10am–5pm). The bulk of the castle was built in the 19th century, giving it a domestic rather than military look. The portrait of the 11th duke's faithful piper, who injured his throat on a grouse bone, was warned never to pipe again, but did so and died, is a highlight. There are also a handful of sketches by Gainsborough in the boudoir. Probably the most atmospheric room is the copper pan-filled Victorian kitchen, which conjures up visions of the sweated and sweating labour required to feed the grandees 'upstairs'. Walled gardens and the extensive grounds hold a treasury of exotic plants, trees and rhododendrons, which command a superb view across the bay. The whole area is a natural playground, with waterfalls, a giant pitcher plant and a maze of paths.

TRNSMT festival

# WHAT TO DO

Wherever you might be staying in Glasgow, there is always something going on, particularly from spring to autumn. Sport, culture, shopping, entertainment and nightlife all feature in abundance. And with proximity to the great outdoors, there are plenty of activities for any weather. Check the VisitScotland website (www.visitscotland.com), where you can also download brochures, for up-to-date information.

ENTERTAINMENT

Most newsagents in Glasgow stock *The List* (www.list.co.uk), a guide to events, theatre, cinema and clubs in UK cities and their surrounding areas, which is published every two months.

LIVE MUSIC AND THEATRE

Glasgow has long had one of the UK's most exciting **music** scenes – indeed, it has produced some of the finest UK bands, such as Franz Ferdinand, Primal Scream and Mogwai – and on any given night you can catch a raft of top-class gigs at some of the best live music venues in Scotland. Major rock bands appear at **Hampden Park** and the **SSE Hydro**. It is said that Oasis were discovered in **King Tut's Wah Wah Club**, an excellent cellar club which is still a fantastic place to see up-and-coming bands.

Other main venues for music in Glasgow are **Òran Mór** and the **Barrowland Ballroom**. The **Glasgow International Jazz Festival** in June brings in jazz musicians from all over the world. **TRNSMT** is a three-day music festival attracting the world's best indie and rock bands to its stages in July each year.

Scottish Youth Theatre

Established in 1976, the Scottish Youth Theatre (Old Sheriff Court, 105 Brunswick Street; tel: 0141-552 3988; http://scottishyouth theatre.org) organises an eclectic programme of classes and performances dedicated to young people, up to 25 years old. Productions are staged in the Brian Cox Studio and theatres around the country.

The redeveloped Theatre Royal is home to the **Scottish Opera**. The Glasgow Royal Concert Hall is the main venue for classical music, with regular concerts by the **Royal Scottish National Orchestra**. The churches in Glasgow regularly host excellent concerts. The prestigious BBC Scottish Symphony Orchestra is based at **City Halls** in Glasgow, taking live music across the country.

Glasgow's first-rate theatres put on high-quality productions all year round. The **Citizens' Theatre** presents serious drama, with more avant-garde shows at the **Tramway** and the **Tron**. More mainstream and family-oriented productions can be seen at **King's Theatre**, while **Theatre Royal** is also known for its musicals. Slightly off the beaten path, **Cottiers Theatre** is also worth checking out.

CLUBS AND PUBS

The liveliest area for nightlife remains the **West End**, with students mixing with locals around Byres Rd, as well as in the nearby Woodlands and Kelvingrove districts. **Argyle Street** is also a great choice for a night out, with a broad selection of excellent pubs, restaurants and cafes. There are countless good pubs dotted throughout the city, in fact, with the whisky bars being a particularly worthwhile jaunt. On Hope Street near Glasgow Central Station, **The Pot Still** is a great option, boasting a bar packed with a couple of hundred bottles of single malt whisky. For those who aren't connoisseurs, the staff are happy to give recommendations.

The city's clubbing scene is rated among the best in the UK, attracting top international DJs and breeding a good deal of local talent. There's a thriving underground scene, while, at the other end of the spectrum, some mega-clubs in this designer-label-conscious city insist on dress codes. Opening hours hover between 11pm to 3am, though some stay open until 5am. Cover charges vary from around £5 during the week up to £25 at the weekend.

SPORTS AND OUTDOOR ACTIVITIES

For all its municipal grandeur and urban chic, this 'dear green place' is surrounded by hills and water and full of things to do. When it comes to sports, there are plenty of ways to experience Glasgow, both from the point of view of a participant and as a spectator.

SPECTATOR SPORTS

Glasgow's five regional football teams are suggestive of the sport's unerring popularity throughout the area. Quite fitting, then, that the country's national football stadium, **Hampden Park**, is located in Southside. Hampden Park is also the home of football club Queen's Park. Glasgow

The Theatre Royal

Warriors are one of Scotland's two professional rugby union sides. They play home games at **Scotstoun Stadium** in the western suburbs of the city. They won the Pro14 (then called Pro12) league title in 2015, becoming the first Scottish rugby union team to win a major trophy. For a Gaelic sport unique to Scotland,

⊙ FOOTBALL IN GLASGOW

Football is one of Glasgow's great passions – and one of its great blights. The most decorated teams in Scottish football, Rangers and Celtic, call Glasgow home. With weekly crowds regularly topping 50,000, they form the 'Old Firm' rivalry that is among the most impassioned of any seen in Britain. They have dominated Scottish football for a century and often play internationally. In 2020 Glasgow will be one of the Euro Championship host cities.

The teams are divided along sectarian lines. Celtic, who play at **Celtic Park** in the eastern district of Parkhead, attract the city's immigrant Irish and Catholic population, while Rangers, based at **Ibrox Stadium** in Govan on the Southside, have traditionally drawn support from the Protestant community. But Glasgow has three other professional teams that should not be overlooked. The Paisley team **St Mirren**, complete the trio of current Glaswegian Scottish Premiership teams, while both **Partick Thistle,** who play at Firhill Stadium in the West End, and **Queen's Park**, residents of Hampden, plod along in the lower reaches of the Scottish league system.

Celtic Celtic Park, Parkhead (www.celticfc.net).
Partick Thistle Firhill Stadium (www.ptfc.co.uk).
Queen's Park Hampden (www.queensparkfc.co.uk).
Rangers Ibrox Stadium, Govan (www.rangers.co.uk).
St Mirren Paisley (www.stmirren.com).

check out **Glasgow Mid Argyll Shinty Club**. Also known as Camanachd, shinty is a fast-paced, athletic game played with sticks and a ball.

GOLF

Scotland is the original home of golf, a powerful lure for visitors wanting to play on the famous links. Many of Scotland's courses are municipal courses open to everyone. To play the famous

Cycling along the canal

courses, it helps to have a letter from your golf club at home stating your experience and handicap. If you choose your hotels or special golfing-holiday package wisely, you can play a different course each day for a week.

The Scots make a distinction between two types of courses: links courses are on or near the sea; parkland (or heathland) courses are inland, often on hilly terrain. The main region near Glasgow for golf, with around eight different clubs, is Troon. It's so popular that there is even an airport at Prestwick mainly serving the demand. **Royal Troon Golf Club** has hosted many a major championship.

BIKING

There are lots of cycle paths around Glasgow and along the Clyde. Within the city, the Glasgow Mountain Bike Circuit in **Pollok Park** has a green circuit for those wanting a gentle ride through the woods, a blue circuit for a bit of bounce and

The Isle Of Bute

climb, and a red circuit for those who want really rugged terrain. You can rent a bike from www.nextbike.co.uk/en/glasgow. For more information about bicycling in Scotland see the VisitScotland website: www.visitscotland.com/see-do/active.

HIKING

Walkers are less than an hour away from the splendours of **Loch Lomond and the Trossachs National Park**, which has Munros, Corbetts, heather hill rambles, forest walks and nature trails that will allow you to glimpse some of the 500 species of flowering plant and 250 species of bird that reside here.

For the really serious outdoors enthusiast, there's the **West Highland Way** to explore, which takes about five to seven days to walk. It takes you from Milngavie, just north of Glasgow, to Fort William, a distance of 96 miles (154km), passing through some of Scotland's most stunning scenery. For information on all the walks that can be done in this area, visit www.lochlomond-trossachs.org.

The Isle of Bute also has its own 30-mile (48-km) hiking route that is listed as one of Scotland's Great Trails. The **West Island Way** (www.westislandway.co.uk) is a pretty, well-maintained route through a surprising array of landscapes, but which is more accessible to less serious hikers thanks to the flatter nature of Bute's topography.

BOATING

Glasgow is a city built on its maritime might, and many marinas and boat clubs line the waterways. Sail out of the **Firth of Clyde** and head north along the shores and you will be astounded by the beauty of the sea lochs, rocky outcrops and inlets, not to mention the isles of Islay and Mull. Experienced **sailors** should visit www.sailscotland.co.uk for information on all the routes, charts, sites, nature and companies that offer boats for hire. For those who can't sail but want to go out on the open waves, the *Waverley* (www.waverleyexcursions.co.uk) is the last remaining seagoing paddle steamer in the world and does summer sails along the Clyde, as well as to the northern lochs and nearby islands of **Arran**, **Bute** and **Cumbrae**. In 2019 it was forced out of service temporarily, so check online for the latest information.

FISHING

One benefit of the demise of heavy industry is that the Clyde is less polluted now, and trout and salmon have returned. **Angling** is becoming increasingly popular on the banks of the rivers of Glasgow. The United Clyde Angling Protective Association Ltd (www.ucapaltd.com) looks after the Clyde and its tributaries, and you can buy a permit from Anglers Attic (tel: 01698-359 757) to fish on a particular stretch.

Safety in the mountains

Despite a concentrated campaign on safety, hikers and mountain climbers continue to get into trouble in Scotland. Always get local advice on weather and conditions. Weather can and often does change rapidly and suddenly, especially in the Trossachs. Be sure you take the proper equipment and let someone know where you are going.

Man playing bagpipes

PONY TREKKING AND RIDING

There are a few horse-riding centres around the outskirts of Glasgow. **Easterton Farm Park** (www.eastertonfarmpark.com) in Milngavie offers lessons, or, if you can already handle a horse, you can hack along the dips and dells of **Mugdock Country Park** in the Campsie Fells, surely one of the most delightful ways to see the scenery.

SKIING & SNOWBOARDING

While Glasgow tends to see less and less snow nowadays, many of the nearby mountains will get a permanent covering during the winter. Nevertheless the best places to strap on some skis in the city is at the artificial slopes. **Snow Factor** (www.snowfactor.com) is an indoor centre that generates real snow, while **Glasgow Ski & Snowboard Centre** (www.ski-glasgow.co.uk) offers outdoor artificial slopes.

BAGPIPING

If you've ever dreamed of mastering the bagpipes, you can learn to pipe at either the **National Piping Centre** (www.thepipingcentre.co.uk), or the **College of Piping** (tel: 0141-334-3587). Evening, day and week-long courses at hugely attractive prices are available during term times throughout the year.

COOKING CLASSES

The **Tennent's Training Academy** (www.tennentstraining academy.co.uk/cookschool) at the Wellpark Brewery offers even the most hopeless cooks a chance to learn how to bring food together in a tasty and attractive way. All sorts of different courses are available, including an afternoon course in Italian cookery (learning how to make gnocchi and delicious sauces among other dishes), and even an afternoon tea masterclass.

SHOPPING

Glasgow is Scotland's major shopping city. Shops are gener- ally open 9am–5.30pm Monday to Saturday (a few places may close on Saturday afternoon), and major shopping centres are also open on Sunday. The main areas are the smart, upmarket **Princes Square**, the **Buchanan Quarter** and **Ingram Street**,

---

⊘ TRACING YOUR ANCESTORS

The excellent Mitchell Library has fabulous, free resources for those looking to research family history or anyone just curious about the city's past. The Family History Section is manned by knowledgeable staff who help people from all over the world delve into records such as the Glasgow newspaper archive (starting in 1715), censuses, war deaths, parish registers and monumental inscriptions.

If you have an ancestor who you know is, or think may be, bur- ied at the Glasgow Necropolis, get in touch with the Friends of Glasgow Necropolis (www.glasgownecropolis.org), who have suc- cessfully mapped much of the graveyard, even managing to dis- cern information from some of the more weathered tombstones.

Authentic Harris tweed

known as Glasgow's 'style mile'. Also popular is the huge glass **St Enoch Centre**.

Almost all merchandise and services are subject to 20 percent Value Added Tax (VAT). For major purchases over a certain amount of money, overseas visitors can get a VAT refund. Note that this applies only to shops that are members of the Retail Export Scheme. When you make your purchase, request a signed form and a stamped pre-addressed envelope; have your form stamped by British Customs as you leave the country and post the form back to the shop to obtain a refund. You can also avoid the VAT if you do your shopping in duty-free shops – look for the sign.

WHAT TO BUY

Kilts and tartans. A number of shops in Glasgow, such as MacGregor & MacDuff, or Hector Russell, specialise in made-to-measure kilts, or full Highland dress. These shops will be glad to help you find your family tartan.

Knitwear and woollens. Scottish knitwear includes cashmere pullovers and cardigans and Shetland and Fair Isle sweaters. Tartan woollens can be bought by the yard, and you can see them woven at several woollen mills. Harris Tweed and sheepskin rugs are also popular buys.

Jewellery. In Glasgow (and elsewhere), look for sterling and enamel jewellery made from the designs of Charles Rennie Mackintosh. Silvercraft from Orkney and Shetland has designs inspired by Norse mythology. Celtic-designed jewellery, clan brooches and ornate kilt pins are often produced in pewter. And for the romantics there's the delicately-worked 'lucken-booth', a traditional Scottish love token.

Whisky. Scotch whisky is not necessarily less expensive in Scotland, but you'll find brands that you never knew existed, so take the opportunity to discover an unusual malt. Glasgow has its own Clyde Distillery, if you'd like to try and buy local.

⊙ THE LOCAL ART SCENE

Despite two devastating fires that ravaged the Charles Rennie Mackintosh-designed Glasgow School of Art (GSA) building, the institution still whirs with the comings and goings of students and artists. It was the home of the influential *fin-de-siècle* Glasgow Group of modern artists – which included Mackintosh – and also boasts celebrated alumni such as Alasdair Gray, Ian Hamilton Finlay, and contemporary artists Jim Lambie, Roddy Buchanan and Simon Starling.

Glasgow's D.I.Y. spirit flourished in the late 1970s and early 1980s, when the city was deep in recession and blighted by sectarian violence. New Glasgow Boys and Girls took over warehouse spaces and set up gallery collectives, the most influential being Transmission in 1983 (www.transmissiongallery.org). By 1996 contemporary art was part of the mainstream and Glasgow got itself a grand building to showcase its artists: The Gallery of Modern Art (GoMA). Arts hubs CCA (Centre for Contemporary Arts), Tramway and Trongate 103 followed.

Art and antiques. The Scottish art scene is an active one. Look for prints and affordable works by young Scottish artists. Victorian antiques and old prints and maps are also a good buy.

ACTIVITIES FOR CHILDREN

Glasgow has attractions and activities for children of all ages. Children enjoy exploring Scottish castles and there are many country parks with wildlife and playgrounds at places like **Kelvingrove Park** is always a good choice. **Queen's Park** has a boating lake and is great for a picnic in summer. There is plenty for children at **Rouken Glen Park** (www.roukenglenpark. co.uk), and it's all free. Two bouncy castles operate in the park (Mar–Oct weekends, public and school hols 11.30am–4.40pm). There are pony rides at 1.30pm in the summer and a children's play area, with multi-sensory area and wheelchair-accessible play equipment, is open year-round.

At **Hampden Park** the Scottish Football Hall of Fame is geared to offer something for kids and adults, along with tours of the stadium. **Kelvingrove Art Gallery and Museum** has enthralling natural history exhibits, and engaging installations like a stuffed elephant and a fighter plane. The refurbished **Summerlee Museum of Scottish Industrial Life** at Coatbridge (tel: 01236-638 460) offers kids the chance to ride on an old tram as part of Scotland's only electric-driven tramway. Also out this way, the **Time Capsule** (tel: 01236-449 572) is worth a visit for the swimming and ice-skating among volcanoes and cavemen.

The Clyde area is also a great spot to take the family. The **Riverside Museum** has plenty of exhibits created with children in mind. The **Tall Ship** is also family-friendly. Across the water, **Glasgow Science Centre** is perhaps Glasgow's finest family-friendly sight.

CALENDAR OF EVENTS

January Celtic Connections, traditional music festival, www.celtic
connections.com. 25 January: Burns Night, Scotland-wide.

February Glasgow Film Festival celebrates the latest local and international contributions to the silver screen (www.glasgowfilm.org).

March Glasgow International Comedy Festival, www.glasgowcomedy
festival.com. The three-week laugh-fest is Europe's largest.

Late April–May Glasgow International Festival (www.glasgowinternational.
org). Biennial which brings together local and international artists in dozens of city-wide spaces, from shop fronts to market stands.

June Music takes over in with the Glasgow International Jazz Festival
(www.jazzfest.co.uk) at various venues including the Old Fruitmarket in
Merchant City. West End Festival, including the Festival Sunday Parade,
also takes place www.westendfestival.co.uk. Glasgow Science Festival
(www.glasgowsciencefestival.org.uk) explores advances in science, technology, medicine and more.

July The eponymous Merchant City Festival (www.merchantcityfestival.
com) is four days of colourful street art, music, theatre, food and drink.
The TRNSMT Festival (https://trnsmt.fest.com) commandeers Glasgow
Green every year.

August World Pipe Band Championships (www.theworlds.co.uk), with
over 200 bands and a whole lot of bagpipes. Pride Glasgow (https://pride
glasgow.com), Scotland's largest LGBTQ festival.

September Doors Open Days, visit the country's best architecture for
free, Scotland-wide, www.doorsopendays.org.uk.

Late October-November The city's main LGBTQ+ event, Glasgay! (www.
outspokenarts.org) covers the whole spectrum of artistic genres.

30 November (and week running up to it): St Andrew's Day.

December 31 Hogmanay, Scotland-wide.

EATING OUT

Given that even in the remotest parts of Scotland the standard of cooking is very high, you can expect to eat well in Glasgow. Scottish chefs have won many accolades at international culinary competitions, and the better hotels may even be staffed by award-winners. The tourist office's 'Taste of Scotland' initiative has encouraged chefs to rethink traditional dishes, using the freshest local ingredients. Chefs make full use of these local specialities: fresh salmon and trout, herring, beef, venison, grouse, pheasant, potatoes, raspberries, and a plethora of other fruit and vegetables.

Much Scottish fare is hearty, intended to warm and insulate against the often frigid weather. Whenever possible, try these traditional dishes, which are often delicious. At the other end of the spectrum, Glasgow accommodates all tastes and diets; vegetarian, and increasingly vegan, options are widely available and the city has restaurants serving cuisine from most conceivable corners of the world, as well as many major chains. The quality is generally very high.

A taste of Scotland

The List's (www.list.co.uk) Eating and Drinking Guide provides listings for Glasgow. For restaurants serving traditional Scottish food visit www.taste-of-scotland.com.

WHEN TO EAT

Like the rest of Scotland, most hotels in Glasgow will provide a continental breakfast (usually between 8am and 10am), with B&Bs often going all-out to cook up a hearty Scottish fry-up to kick-start the day. Restaurants usually serve lunch from around noon until 2.30pm, although some, especially pubs, will keep the kitchen open until late. High tea is generally more than just an afternoon snack, and can be quite filling. It is usually served from 2 to 5pm. Dinner is usually available at all restaurants between 6 and 10pm, but many serve later on weekends. There are lots of good options serving pre-theatre menus near the main theatres.

Arbroath smokies

In general, restaurant prices compare favourably with those south of the border. This does not prevent certain Glaswegian establishments from charging prices that would not be out of place in London's West End. Keep in mind the inclusion in restaurant prices of 20 percent VAT sales tax, and often a 10 percent service charge.

WHAT TO EAT

Breakfast

A Scottish breakfast is a mini event in itself. Porridge is served with cream or milk, followed by fruit juice, fresh fruit, eggs, sausage, bacon, tomatoes, mushrooms, potato scones, rolls, jam and marmalade. A special touch could be the addition of Scottish kipper or smoked haddock. The famous Arbroath 'smokies' are salted haddock flavoured with hot birch or oak smoke. Haggis is occasionally included. Vegetarians are increasingly catered for, with vegetarian substitutes, including vegetarian haggis, available, especially on prior notice.

Soups and Broths

Traditional Scottish soups are best if they are homemade. Try a few of the following:

Cock-a-leekie: a seasoned broth made from boiling fowl with leeks and sometimes onions and prunes. Consumed for at least 400 years and dubbed the national soup of Scotland.

Partan bree: creamed crab (partan) soup.

Scotch broth: a variety of vegetables in a barley-thickened soup with mutton or beef.

Cullen skink: milky broth of Finnan haddock with onions and potatoes.

Lorraine: a creamy chicken soup made with nutmeg, almonds and lemon, named after Mary of Guise-Lorraine.

Oatmeal: made with onion, leek, carrot and turnip.

Main Courses

Fish and shellfish. Scottish smoked salmon is famous all over the world, thanks to the distinct flavours introduced by the unique peat or oak-chip smoking process. Farmed salmon is now widely available, and while the purist may argue that it isn't as good as the wild variety, there are few people who can actually tell the difference. Nothing is better than a whole fresh Scottish salmon poached with wine and vegetables. The west coast produces excellent lobster, scallops, crayfish, mussels and oysters.

Meat and game. Scottish beef rivals the best in Europe. Aberdeen Angus steak is a favourite, typically served with a mushroom-and-wine sauce. Whisky goes into many sauces served with beef: Gaelic steak, for instance, is seasoned with garlic and fried with sautéed onions, with whisky added during the cooking process. *Forfar bridies* are pastry puffs stuffed with minced steak and onions. If you are lucky, you might also find beef collops (slices) in pickled walnut sauce.

Game still abounds in Scotland. After the shooting season opens (on August 12th), grouse is an expensive but much sought-after dish, served in a pie or roasted with crispy bacon and served with bread sauce or fried breadcrumbs. Venison appears frequently on menus, often roasted or in a casserole. You will also find pheasant, guinea fowl, quail and hare in terrines, pâtés and game pies.

Haggis. Haggis, Scotland's national dish, hardly deserves its grisly reputation among non-Scots. Properly made, it consists

Homemade haggis

Single-malt whisky

of chopped-up sheep's offal, oatmeal, onions, beef suet and seasoning, boiled in a sewn-up sheep's stomach. Haggis is traditionally accompanied by 'chappit tatties' and 'bashed neeps' – mashed potatoes and turnips.

Potatoes and oatmeal. Potatoes are a particular source of local pride. 'Stovies' are leftovers from a Sunday roast, usually including potatoes, onions, carrots, gravy and occasionally the meat, cooked in the dripping. 'Rumbledethumps' are a mix of boiled cabbage and mashed potatoes (sometimes with onions or chives and grated cheese added). You won't need to go all the way to northernmost Caithness for Scotland's basic dish of 'tatties' (potatoes boiled in their skin) and herrings, where they are a speciality. A typical Orkney Island dish is 'clapshot' (potatoes and turnips mashed together and seasoned with fresh black pepper) to accompany their haggis. 'Skirlie' is a mixture of oatmeal and onions flavoured with thyme and oatmeal also turns up as a coating on such foods as herring and cheese, as well as in desserts.

Other traditional dishes are 'Scotch eggs': hard-boiled eggs wrapped in sausage meat and coated in breadcrumbs, deep-fried and eaten hot or cold, and 'Scotch woodcock': toast topped with anchovy and scrambled egg.

Afternoon Tea and Dessert

Glasgow has plenty of tearooms offering afternoon tea, complete with sandwiches, cakes and other delicacies. Shortbread is, of course, a Scottish speciality. Another classic Scottish favourite is rich, dark Dundee cake, made with dried fruits and spices, topped with almonds. Scones and 'bannocks' (oatmeal cakes) are among the great array of Scottish baked and griddled goods. A teatime treat is Scotch pancakes, served with butter and marmalade or honey. Oatcakes come either rough or smooth and they are eaten on their own or with butter, pâté, jam, or 'crowdie', Scotland's centuries-old version of cottage cheese. In Glasgow, don't miss going to Mackintosh at the Willow, the original Charles Rennie Mackintosh-designed tearoom.

For dessert, you'll see various combinations of cheese, with red berries or black cherries and vanilla ice cream. Cranachan, a tasty Scottish speciality, consists of toasted oatmeal and cream and whisky or rum topped with nuts and raspberries or other soft fruit. Rhubarb-and-ginger tart is worth looking out for, as is butterscotch tart.

Whisky drinking

Purists insist that a single-malt whisky should be drunk only neat or with a few drops of water – never with mixers. Ice is frowned upon; asking to add soda water might get you banned from the bar. Both are more acceptable with blended Scotch though.

Scotland produces several excellent varieties of cheddar cheese and recent years have seen a rediscovery of old Scottish cheeses. Produced (although on a small scale) throughout the country, the speciality cheeses are characterised by a high degree of individuality. Try Criffel, Lanark blue, Isle of Mull or creamy Crannog or Orkney Cheddar.

WHAT TO DRINK

A huge amount of folklore surrounds every aspect of **Scotch whisky**, from its distillation using pure mountain water, to the aroma of the peat, to its storage, all the way to the actual drinking. The word 'whisky' derives from the Gaelic *uisge beatha* 'water of life'. It is available in two basic types – *malt* (distilled solely from malted barley) and *grain* (made from malted barley and grain). Most of the Scotch sold today is blended, combining malt and grain whiskies. There are now more than 2,000 brands of authentic Scotch whisky.

Single malt whiskies are considered to be of the highest pedigree. There are six whisky producing regions of Scotland:

⊙ GLASGOW'S HISTORIC PUBS

Some of Glasgow's grand old buildings are now devoted to the Glaswegian passion for having a 'blether' over a drink. The Counting House on the corner of George Square has been converted into a pub and restaurant with splendid interior statuary, cornicing and a glass dome above the bar; The Auctioneers in North Court is furnished with the kind of bric-a-brac that used to pass through McTear's auction showrooms; and The Drum & Monkey is beautifully lit by the vaulted windows of a former bank, with thick marble columns and lofty carved ceilings.

Grand interior at The Counting House

Highlands, Islands, Lowlands, Speyside, Campbeltown and Islay. Two of the most distinctive are Speyside (mellower and floral) and Islay (peaty and occasionally medicinal).

Scotland's version of Irish coffee, which naturally uses local whisky, may be called a 'Gaelic coffee'. A 'Rusty Nail' is one measure of malt whisky plus one measure of Drambuie. A 'Scotch Mist' is made from whisky, squeezed lemon rind and crushed ice. An 'Atholl Brose' blends oatmeal, heather honey and whisky.

Scotland is proud of its **beer**. The Scottish equivalent of English 'bitter' is called 'heavy', and should be served at room temperature. The 'half and a half' featured in old-fashioned pubs is a dram of whisky with a half pint of beer as a chaser. Tennents is the main lager in Glasgow, but there are plenty of good craft beer options too, like the offerings of Drygate and West breweries. Good quality wine is widely available in restaurants and bars.

PLACES TO EAT

We have used the following symbols to give an idea of the price for a 3-course meal for one person without wine or service.

££££	over £50
£££	£35–£50
££	£25–£35
£	under £25

CENTRAL GLASGOW & MERCHANT CITY

The 13th Note £ *50–60 King St, tel: 0141-553 1638,* www.13thnote.co.uk. Vegetarian and vegan food with Greek and other Mediterranean influences in one of Glasgow's hippest restaurants on arty King St. Mains include pan-fried lemongrass and ginger rice cakes in red Thai curry sauce, and a veggie haggis with neeps and tatties. Open daily for lunch and dinner.

Babbity Bowster ££ *16–18 Blackfriars Street, tel: 0141-552 5055,* www. babbitybowster.com. The popular downstairs café-bar serves seafood and Scottish fare with a French influence, but for a quieter, more intimate dinner, it's advisable to eat upstairs in the charming dining room (dinner only Fri & Sat). You can stay here too, but it can sometimes be very noisy. Open daily for lunch and dinner.

Brian Maule at Le Chardon d'Or ££££ *176 West Regent St, tel: 0141-248 3801,* www.brianmaule.com. Owner-chef Maule, who worked with the Roux brothers at *Le Gavroche* in London, turns out fancy but unpretentious French-influenced food along the lines of assiette of pork with creamed potatoes and truffle jus. Open Tue–Sat for lunch and dinner.

Café Gandolfi ££ *64 Albion St, tel: 0141-552 6813,* www.cafegandolfi.com. Designed with distinctive wooden furniture from the Tim Stead workshop, *Café Gandolfi* serves up a wonderful selection of Scottish-inspired dishes, such as Stornoway black pudding, peat-smoked salmon and seared Barra scallops with Stornoway black pudding. The snappy little attic bar offers the same food daily plus a cracking little pizza menu; great gin card too. Open daily for lunch and dinner (bar opens for lunch and dinner only).

Gamba £££ *225a West George St, tel: 0141-572 0899,* www.gamba.co.uk. Continental contemporary sophistication prevails in this super basement restaurant where fish is king: once you've devoured the signature fish soup – a delicious mix with Portland crabmeat and prawn dumplings – perhaps try some seared king scallops with creamed celeriac and black pudding. A beautifully refined interior and outstanding service. The lunch menu is good value and there's a pre-theatre deal too. Open Mon–Sat for lunch and dinner & Sun for dinner.

La Lanterna ££ *35 Hope Street, tel: 0141-221 9160,* https://lalanterna -glasgow.co.uk. This small, unpretentious establishment serves Italian cuisine in elegant rustic surroundings. The restaurant prides itself on the authenticity and excellence of its cuisine. The pre-theatre menu is excellent value. Open Mon–Sat for lunch and dinner.

Mackintosh at the Willow £ *215 Sauchiehall Street, tel: 0141-204 1903,* www.mackintoshatthewillow.com. This is the real deal. Mackintosh designed every aspect of this tearoom, right down to the spoons, for restaurateur Kate Cranston at the turn of the 20th century. The afternoon tea is great value. There is also a pre-theatre menu, a good option for matinees. A recreated Willow Tea Rooms can also be found on Buchanan Street. Open daily for breakfast, lunch afternoon tea.

Mono ££ *12 Kings Court, tel: 0141-553 2400,* www.monocafebar.com. This unassuming, multi-functional venue combines a fully vegan restaurant, bar and indie CD shop all within an airy space. Mains include tofu, beansprout and tenderstem broccoli noodles with gado gado dressing, and there's a superb selection of craft beer and organic wine. There are regular gigs (alternative, rock) too. Open daily for lunch and dinner.

Mussel Inn ££ *157 Hope St, tel: 0141-572 1405,* www.mussel-inn.com. This busy, buzzy restaurant, with high ceilings and aquamarine-painted walls, concentrates on simply-prepared pots of fresh mussels, grilled or chilled oysters, grilled queen scallops with garlic butter, and other delights from the sea. For the 'lunchtime quickie' menu, you get a bowl of mussels with a choice of sauce and chips, or seafood chowder with salad or chips. Open daily for lunch and dinner.

Paesano Pizza £ *94 Miller St, tel: 0141-258 5565,* www.paesanopizza. co.uk. In a city bursting with great Italian restaurants, this authentic, hugely popular Neapolitan pizzeria is a real standout. Cooked in wood-fired ovens made in Naples, there are nine different pizzas to choose from, each one made using a hybrid yeast and sourdough recipe and with the freshest Italian ingredients. Open daily for lunch and dinner.

The Red Onion ££ *257 West Campbell Street, tel: 0141-221 6000,* www. red-onion.co.uk. Dishes here are modern twists on classic Scottish cooking, all delicately prepared. There are various set menus available including the pre-theatre, vegan, dairy-free and gluten-free options. The spacious and relaxed space has mixed seating, including booths and a mezzanine. Open daily lunch and dinner.

Sarti ££ *133 Wellington St, tel: 0141-248 2228,* www.fratelli-sarti.co.uk. The Sarti brothers' flagship Italian café and restaurant – at Wellington St – remains as authentic and as popular as ever, with pizzas and *primi* piatti for around £12; the breakfast club (8–11am) is great fun. The slightly more formal dining space is accessed from the Bath St entrance. Open Mon–Sat for breakfast, lunch and dinner & Sun for lunch and dinner.

Windows ££ *In the Carlton George, 44 West George Street, 7th floor, tel: 0141-353 6373,* www.carlton.nl/george. An excellent and attractive restaurant with fabulous rooftop views. Only the freshest produce is used in dishes that celebrate Scottish cuisine. It is advisable to book ahead. Open daily for lunch and dinner.

WEST END

Balbir's ££ *7 Church St, tel: 0141-339 7711,* www.balbirs.co.uk. Owner Balbir Singh Sumal is one of the city's long-standing curry kings, and this striking-looking restaurant – with its capacious, darkened interior – features his wholesome approach to affordable Indian cuisine. The menu features dishes such as lamb *karahi* and okra fries. Open daily for dinner.

The Bothy ££ *11 Ruthven Lane, tel: 0141-334 4040, www.bothyglasgow. co.uk.* Set in a lovely 1870s stone mansion, this place has a cosy interior and bench seating in the cobbled yard outside. The emphasis here is firmly on Scottish flavours, for example Isle of Arran haggis and beer-battered Scrabster haddock with hand-cut chips and mushy peas. Open daily for lunch and dinner.

Crabshakk £££ *1114 Argyle St, tel: 0141-334 6127, www.crabshakk.com.* Fantastic little restaurant serving up an array of superb Scottish sea-food. There's an ever-changing line-up of specials, as well as some un-missable stalwarts such as scallops served in a sizzling, caramelised anchovy sauce. You can also splash out on a shellfish platter for two. Open daily for lunch and dinner.

The Dockyard Social £ *95–107 Haugh Rd, www.dockyardsocial.com.* Taking over a vast warehouse in Finnieston, this street food hub has the local community at its heart with an inspiring three-pronged ambition to showcase the best of Glasgow's food scene, support start-up food businesses, and help Glasgow's most disadvantaged people through a professional culinary training school. Open Sat & sun for lunch and dinner, Fri for dinner.

Eusebi ££ *152 Park Rd, tel: 0141-648 9999, www.eusebideli.com.* Cheery, family-run enterprise that has been doling out a veritable cornucopia of foodie treats for forty years: hand-made pasta straight out of the *pastaficio*, cured meats from the *salumeria* and delectable-looking cannoli in the cabinets; the venison *ragu* pappardelle shouldn't be missed. With its floor-to-ceiling windows and bold red and white livery, *Eusebi* has a great feel to it too. Open daily for breakfast, lunch and dinner.

The Hanoi Bike Shop ££ *8 Ruthven Lane, tel: 0141-334 7165, www. hanoibikeshop.co.uk.* This colourful place just off the busy Byres Rd might not have much to do with bicycles (though there are wheels on the walls), but it is just the ticket for a quick hit of Vietnamese street food from salt and chilli squid, to steaming bowls of *pho*. There's a vegan menu and lots of gluten free options. Open daily for lunch and dinner.

Number 16 £££ *16 Byres Rd, tel: 0141-339 2544,* www.number16.co.uk. Intimate, wood-beamed establishment covering two floors, with daily changing menus to reflect the best Scottish produce. Mains might include the likes of pork belly with Hispi cabbage and heritage carrots. Open daily for lunch and dinner.

Òran Mór ££ *Top of Byres Rd, at Great Western Rd, tel: 0141-357 6200,* www.oran-mor.co.uk. Multi-purpose arts venue that comprises a bar with over 250 malt whiskies, two restaurants, a club and a private event space, all within the beautifully restored Kelvinside Parish Church. Perhaps the best reason to visit, though, is for the perennially popular *A Play, A Pie and A Pint*, a self-explanatory lunchtime theatre programme. Open daily for breakfast, lunch and dinner.

Ox and Finch ££ *920 Sauchiehall Street, tel: 0141-339 8627,* www.oxand finch.com. In a trendy part of town, this sharing-plate restaurant offers relaxed and rustic fine dining. The menu consists of a selection of tapas dishes and the dining area is bright and open. Open daily lunch and dinner.

Stravaigin ££ *28 Gibson St, tel: 0141-334 2665,* www.stravaigin.co.uk. This gorgeous basement restaurant and hip street-level café-bar combination offers exciting dining. Utilizing a host of unexpected ingredients, the results are unusual and wildly inventive combinations such as ox tongue, *baba ganoush*, cracked-wheat risotto and shallot crisp to start, followed by truffled celeriac and potato gratin with wild mushrooms, shaved chestnut and fermented cabbage. Open daily for lunch and dinner.

Two Fat Ladies at The Buttery £££ *652 Argyle St, tel: 0141-221 8188,* www.twofatladiesrestaurant.com. The *Two Fat Ladies* has been in business for over twenty-five years and their two restaurants are favourites of Glasgow's fish lovers. Heavy on fresh Scottish seafood, there are daily changing fish platters alongside regulars like flash-fried West Coast scallops, crispy gnocchi, wild mushrooms and cheddar cream. Open daily for lunch and dinner.

The Ubiquitous Chip £££ *12 Ashton Lane, tel: 0141-334 5007*, www. ubiquitouschip.co.uk. Opened in 1971, the *Chip* led the way in headlining high-end modern Scottish cuisine, and it's still going strong today. There's fine dining in the foliage-entwined courtyard or more informal brasserie food upstairs, but either way, expect mouth-watering plates like guinea fowl breast with medjool date and harissa. Open daily for lunch and dinner.

Wee Curry Shop ££ *29 Ashton Lane, tel: 0141 357 5280*, www.weecurry shopglasgow.co.uk. Tiny but welcoming place near the Glasgow Film Theatre and Sauchiehall St shops (there's also a branch in the West End on Ashton Lane), serving home-made bargain meals to compete with the best in town. Expect the likes of chicken curry and smoked aubergines with potatoes and okra, to eat-in or take away. There's a speedy two-course lunch menu served from noon until 2pm. Open daily for lunch and dinner.

Wee Lochan £££ *340 Crow Rd, tel: 0141-338 6606*, www.an-lochan.com. If you want the best in fresh, unadulterated west-coast Scottish fish, there are few better places in Glasgow, although it is off the beaten track, in the Jordanhill district. Typical mains include salmon *en-croute*, and pan-seared sea bass fillets with baby squid and tiger prawns. They also do non-fish dishes and a great all-day Sunday lunch. Open Mon–Sat for lunch and dinner & Sun for roast dinners until 7pm.

EAST END

A'Challtainn BAaD ££ *54 Calton Entry, tel: 0141-548 1338*, www.baad glasgow.com. Set in BAaD's airy atrium, the restaurant boasts a beautiful plant-strewn interior of wood floors and muted greys. The food focuses on sustainable Scottish seafood with mains like Shetland *moules* *marinère* and Scottish lobster with garlic butter and seaweed fries. Open Tue–Sun for lunch and dinner.

Celino's Alexandra Parade ££ *620 Alexandra Parade, tel: 0141-554 0523,* www.celinos.com. Plucked straight out of Rome, this spot is packed with character. All sorts of meat products hand from the ceiling and the space is separated into a bustling delicatessen café and a more laid-back restaurant. This is the original Celino's, open since 1982, and has remained a family-run enterprise ever since. Open Mon–Sat for breakfast, lunch and dinner, Sun for lunch and dinner.

Drygate ££ *85 Drygate, tel: 0141-212 8815,* www.drygate.com. Drygate has crafted a fine space in the side of its brewery. The ground-floor Brasserie is separated from the brewing process by plate glass windows, so you can observe the brewing as you dine. There's also an upstairs Beer Hall leading to a rooftop terrace. The brasserie menu is heavy on the comfort food, with brisket burgers, steak frites and *poutine* sides setting the tone. Open daily for lunch and dinner.

SOUTHSIDE

Art Lovers' Café £ *House for an Art Lover, Bellahouston Park, tel: 0141-483 1611,* www.houseforanartlover.co.uk. Whether you're visiting the house or not, the dining room in this showcase house is well worth making the effort to get to; both light lunches and full meals are served, for example smoked haddock rarebit on toasted sourdough with leeks and poached eggs and chargrilled flat iron steak on toasted ciabatta; afternoon tea (best booked in advance) is served 2–4pm. Lovely garden views too. Open daily for lunch and afternoon tea.

The Fish People Café ££ *350a Scotland St, tel: 0141-429 8787,* www.thefishpeoplecafe.co.uk. Ignore the wholly unappealing location (right outside the subway station on a dismal main road): this fish restaurant is top drawer. Take your pick from any number of excellent dishes, like crisp-fried stone bass, black tiger prawn, wilted spinach and spiced ginger cream, or just perch at the marble-topped bar with a plate of Cumbrae rock oysters. Open Tue–Sat for lunch and dinner & Sun for lunch.

La Fiorentina £ *2 Paisley Rd West, tel: 0141-420 1585*, www.la-fiorentina.com. A critics' favourite which also tops popular surveys, this Tuscan-influenced restaurant has become an institution. The lengthy menu features the like of pan-fried veal medallions with a white wine sauce and Parma ham. Open Tue–Sun for lunch and dinner.

A–Z TRAVEL TIPS

A SUMMARY OF PRACTICAL INFORMATION

A

ACCOMMODATION

There is a huge variety of accommodation in Glasgow: hotels, boutiques, guest houses, hostels, bed-and-breakfasts, campus accommodation (in summer), and even a few manor houses. The Scottish Tourist Board inspects and grades many of these establishments. There are also hundreds of self-catering cottages. The tourist board VisitScotland (www.visitscotland.com) can supply information about all these options and even help with booking. Check online for an e-brochure listing some of the options available.

Hotels vary greatly in standards, from world class five-star suites to basic rooms with only basic amenities. Some hotels have swimming pools, and further out of the city, quite a few have their own golf courses. Book ahead for Easter, and June–September, and especially during some of the bigger festivals, when prices can rise quite significantly. Hogmanay (December and early January) is another busy time. If you do find yourself in Glasgow without a reservation, head to the nearest VisitScotland office, where staff can usually find a bed for you.

Guest houses and bed-and-breakfast (B&B) premises can be great bargains, although you'll sometimes have to share a bathroom. Most establishments have a restaurant or can arrange for an evening meal.

AIRPORTS

Glasgow has one major airport and two more nearby in Prestwick and Edinburgh. They all serve international flights, while many regional domestic airports scattered about on the mainland and the islands are served by Loganair.

Glasgow Airport (www.glasgowairport.com) handles much of Scotland's air traffic. It is a 9-mile (15km), 20-minute taxi or bus ride from the city centre. Buses, including the Glasgow Airport Express, travel every 10–30 minutes between the airport and Buchanan bus station in central Glasgow. Buses from the Buchanan station travel to Edinburgh (about 70 minutes) and other destinations in Scotland.

Prestwick Airport (www.glasgowprestwick.com), about one hour from Glasgow (32 miles/51km), handles European flights. The modern terminal has its own train station, with services to Glasgow approximately every 20 minutes. Public buses run to Glasgow and destinations in Ayrshire.

Edinburgh Airport (www.edinburghairport.com) handles UK, European and transatlantic services, and is beginning to rival Glasgow in the number of international flights it receives. The airport is 7 miles (11km) from Edinburgh, and is linked with Waverley railway station at Waverley Bridge, in the city centre by a special Airlink bus service that leaves every 10 minutes and takes about 30 minutes. A tram also runs from the airport to the city (York Place). Taxis are available just outside the arrival hall.

B

BICYCLE HIRE

Glasgow offers many fine cycling opportunities and some dedicate cycle lanes away from the roads. Due to the steep nature of the streets in the centre of the city, it is not easy to amble around on a bicycle though. Local firms rent bicycles by the hour, day, or week. VisitScotland lists many rental firms on their website (www.visitscotland.com). Book ahead for July or August. For more information on cycling in the city, as well as a list of the dedicated cycle routes, visit https://peoplemakeglasgow.com/cycling-in-glasgow.

BUDGETING FOR YOUR TRIP

Although good value for money is still the general rule in Glasgow, bargains are rare and prices tend to be higher during popular times of the year. Here are a few guidelines to help with budget planning:

Accommodation: A double room in a moderately priced hotel with breakfast tends to cost £50–70 per person. A double per person in a guest house with breakfast will be more like £40–60. Bed-and-breakfast (without bath), £35–50 per person.

Meals: Lunch in pub or café £8–15; Three-course dinner in a moderate restaurant with wine: £25-30 per person; afternoon tea £7; a pint of beer ranges from £2.70–4.

Airport transfer: Glasgow airport: bus (Glasgow Express) £8 (£12 return), taxi £25.

Bicycle hire: £20–25 per day, £70–90 per week.

Buses: Edinburgh–Glasgow (standard tickets) £7.90 (£10 return). Explorer Pass: 3 days £49; 5 days £74, or 8 days £99; www.citylink.co.uk. City and local buses: fares can depend on distance. Minimum bus fares in Glasgow start at £1.60; exact fare in cash is required, although some buses now accept contactless payments.

Campsites: £15–25 per tent per night.

Shopping: Pure wool tartan, about £46 per metre; cashmere scarf, from around £35; kilt: man's from £250, woman's from £125; cashmere sweater from £100; lambswool sweater £25–40.

Sights: Most museums in Glasgow are free. Other sites range from around £4-13 per person.

Taxis: Basic rate for two passengers in Glasgow begins at £3.30 until 11pm, then £4.40 until 6am; price increases by 75p every kilometre. Many hotels have a taxi call button in the lobby.

Tours: City on-and-off bus tours from £14.40; Clyde cruises from one hour to full day £12–40.

Trains: Prices vary according to day or time of travel. Glasgow–Edinburgh £12.90 off-peak travel one way. Spirit of Scotland pass (accepted on trains, buses and most ferries): 8 days (4 days of travel) £139, 15 days (8 days of travel) £179. Saver one-way fares (on ScotRail services only and bought at least one day in advance): London–Edinburgh £70.50; Edinburgh–Inverness £22.50; Glasgow–Aberdeen £10; Wemyss Bay rail and sail ferry/train combo ticket for Bute £11.05 one way; www.scotrail.co.uk.

C

CAR HIRE

If you plan to spend most of the time in Glasgow's compact city centre then a car might be more of a burden than a boon. However travelling to many places in the south and west of the city is much simpler with a car, as are day trips to the surrounding areas. As a rule, it is cheaper to book a hire car before you leave on your trip. Be sure to check whether your credit card covers insurance. A medium-sized compact family car will cost around £240 per week, £48 per day, including VAT, unlimited mileage, but not insurance. Prices vary widely according to season. Beware hidden extras.

To hire a car you must be 21 or more years of age and have held a driver's licence for at least 12 months. The only exception to the latter point at the time of writing was Enterprise, who will hire to somebody who has passed their test in the last 12 months providing they are over 30. Valid drivers' licences from almost all countries are recognised by the British authorities.

Many major car rental companies have their main desks at Glasgow airport, including: Avis, tel: 0844-581 0147, www.avis.co.uk; Budget, tel: 0344-544 4604, www.budget.co.uk; Europcar, tel: 0371 384 1079, www.europcar.co.uk; Enterprise, tel: 0141-830 1300, www.enterprise.co.uk; Hertz, tel: 0843-309 3031, www.hertz.co.uk. For competitive rates, try Arnold Clark, tel: 0141-237 4374, www.arnoldclarkrental.com.

CLIMATE

Scotland has a temperate climate influenced by the Atlantic Ocean, which brings plenty of rain over western Scotland, from which Glasgow is not immune. Summers are warm and wet; winters are cold and wet. The best months to visit are May and June, which have the most hours of sunshine and comparatively little rain. Midges and other stinging insects become a serious problem, especially around lochs outside the city on the west coast, in full summer.

Average monthly temperatures are as follows:

	J	F	M	A	M	J	J	A	S	O	N	D
°C	4	5	7	10	14	17	19	18	15	11	7	6
°F	39	41	44	50	58	62	66	64	59	52	44	43

CLOTHING

Even if you're holidaying in Glasgow in midsummer, take warm clothing and rainwear. Anoraks are very useful: buy a bright colour to make yourself conspicuous to hunters if you're going to be hiking or climbing. Sturdy shoes are a must both for outdoor walking and an umbrella will likely prove itself useful at some point.

Scotland makes some of the world's best clothing, and you'll find a fine selection of knits, woollens and tweeds, although not at significantly lower prices than elsewhere in the UK.

CRIME AND SAFETY

As with any large city, crime in Glasgow can be a problem, but even though the city has Scotland's highest crime rate, it is not dangerous by world, or even most European standards. Take all the usual precautions. Any loss of theft must be reported immediately to the police to comply with your travel insurance rules. Always travel with travel insurance. Honesty, however, is still quite prevalent, even in cities like Glasgow.

CUSTOMS AND ENTRY REQUIREMENTS (SEE VISAS)

D

DRIVING

If you are bringing your own car or one from Europe you will need the registration papers and insurance coverage, along with the more obvious driver's license. Overseas visitors driving their own cars will need Green Card insurance as well.

Road conditions. A limited number of motorways connect Glasgow and Edinburgh with other major cities and areas. Be aware that most A roads are winding, two-lane roads, often skirting Scotland's many lochs and they can be slow-going. A surprise to most visitors are the single-lane roads found in the hinterland and on the islands. Most of these are paved, with passing places for giving way to oncoming traffic or allowing cars behind you to overtake (thank the driver who pulls over for you). Obviously, you should never park in these essential passing places. The twisting roads, along with the need for pulling in and out of the side slips, will more than double your normal driving time even over short distances. Other obstacles include sheep and cattle that often wander onto minor roads. Signposting is adequate, but a good map is essential.

Rules and regulations. The same basic rules apply in all of Britain. Drive on the left, overtake on the right. Turn left on a roundabout (traffic circle), but give way to the right; at a junction where no road has priority, yield to traffic coming from the right. Seat belts must be worn. Drinking and driving is regarded as a serious offence and penalties are severe, involving loss of licence, heavy fines, and even prison sentences, and the law is strictly enforced.

Speed limits. In built-up areas, 30 or 40mph (48 or 65kmh), although residential areas enforce the 20mph limit (32kmh); on major roads, 60mph (96kmh); on dual carriageways and motorways, 70mph (112kmh).

Fuel. Petrol is sold by the Imperial gallon (about 20 percent more voluminous than the US gallon) and by the litre; pumps show both measures. Four-star grade is 97 octane and three-star is 94 octane. Unleaded petrol and diesel is widely available. Most petrol stations are self-service. In the more remote areas stations are rather scarce, so take advantage when you see one.

Roadside assistance. Members of automobile clubs that are affiliated with the British Automobile Association (AA) or the Royal Automobile Club (RAC) can benefit from speedy, efficient assistance in the event of a breakdown. If this should happen to you, AA members should tel: 0800-887 766, RAC members tel: 0800-828 282. Green Flag Motoring Assistance, tel: 0800-051 0636.

Parking. There are meters in major centres and vigilant corps of traffic police and wardens to ticket violators, even in small towns. Ticket machines take most coins and some now take credit cards. Do not park on double yellow lines. In central Glasgow, unless your hotel offers parking, your car is best left in a car park. Concert Square, next to Buchanan bus station has a large multi-storey car park.

Road signs. Many standard international picture signs are displayed in Scotland. Distances are shown in miles. In the Highlands and islands only, road signs may appear first in Gaelic, then English.

E

ELECTRICITY

Throughout Scotland it's 230 volts AC, 50 Hz. Certain appliances may need a converter. Americans will need an adapter.

EMBASSIES AND CONSULATES

Many countries have consuls or other representatives in Edinburgh, but others only have representation in London.

Australia: Australian High Commission, Australia House, Strand, London WC2B 4LA, tel: 020-7379 4334.

Canada: Canada House, Trafalgar Square, London, SW1Y 5BJ; tel: 020-7004 6000

Ireland: 16 Randolph Crescent, Edinburgh, EH3 7TT; tel: 0131-226 7711

New Zealand: 5 Rutland Square, Edinburgh, EH1 2AX; tel: 0131-222 8109

South Africa: South Africa House, Trafalgar Square, London, WC2N 5DP; tel: 020-7451 7299

US: American Consulate General, 3 Regent Terrace, Edinburgh EH7 5BW; tel: 0131-556 8315.

EMERGENCIES

To call the fire brigade, police, ambulance, coast guard, lifeboat, or mountain rescue service, dial 999 from any telephone. You don't need a coin. Tell the emergency operator which service you need.

G

GETTING THERE

By air.

From North America. Direct transatlantic flights to Glasgow from Toronto are offered by Air Canadian Rouge and Air Transat. WestJet fly from Halifax. Delta Air Lines fly from New York JFK and United from Newark. Virgin Atlantic fly to Orlando. Flights from a variety of US hubs route flights via London or Amsterdam.

From Australia and New Zealand. Qantas offer non-direct flights from Sydney and Melbourne to London. Air New Zealand has daily flights to London from Auckland. Onward flights to Glasgow are available with a large number of operators.

From England and Republic of Ireland. There are direct services from all parts of the UK on British Airways, Flybe and easyJet including frequent departures from Birmingham, Heathrow, Gatwick, Stansted, Southampton, Bristol and Manchester. Aer Lingus and Ryanair have regular flights from Dublin. Loganair connects Glasgow to a number of outlying airports around Scotland, including Barra, Islay and Kirkwall.

From Europe. Air France, KLM, Lufthansa, Ryanair and easyJet have direct flights from continental Europe to either Glasgow, Edinburgh or Aberdeen.

Air fares. The highest air fares are from June to September; fares in other months of the year may be considerably lower. All airlines offer economy fares: APEX, etc. These are subject to restrictions – for example, APEX flights have to be booked at least 14 days in advance and tickets are not refundable.

From the US, a direct flight to London with a domestic flight to Glasgow may be the cheapest option. Many American airlines offer a variety of package deals, both for group travel and for those who wish to travel independently. Packages include airfare, accommodation and travel between holiday destinations and may include some meals.

By rail. The train journey from London Euston to Glasgow takes around

5 hours. A sleeper service is available from London (Euston) to Glasgow. Economy fares are offered.

Visitors can take advantage of a variety of special fare plans that operate in Scotland. The **Spirit of Scotland Travelpass** is available for either 4 days of travel over 8 consecutive days, or 8 days of travel over 15 consecutive days. The pass gives unlimited travel on many bus routes and Caledonian MacBrayne (www.calmac.co.uk) ferries as well as on Scotland's rail network. Travelpass holders can obtain a 20 percent reduction on NorthLink sailings from Aberdeen or Stromness to Orkney and Shetland. It can be purchased at ScotRail stations or online (www.scotrail.co.uk), and at selected English travel centres. You can also choose from a selection of Rail Rover tickets; enquire at railway stations.

Visitors from abroad who wish to tour by rail can buy a **BritRail Pass** (www.britrail.net) before leaving their home countries. These offer unlimited travel on the railway network throughout Scotland, England and Wales during a consecutive period of 3, 4, 8, 15, 22 days, or a month. The **Flexipass** allows journeys to be made on non-consecutive days; for example, 4 days unlimited travel over a month period. Children aged 5 to 15 pay half price. The **BritRail Youth Pass** is for youngsters aged 16–25. None of these can be purchased in Britain.

By road. From London the quickest route is to take the M1 north to connect with the M6 and eventually the M74. If you are in the west, the M5 merges with the M6 and connects with the M74.

There are frequent coach services from all over Britain to various Scottish destinations by **National Express** (www.nationalexpress.com) and **Scottish Citylink** (www.citylink.co.uk).

By sea. Ferry services from Northern Ireland operate from Larne to Cairnryon and Belfast to Stranraer.

GUIDES AND TOURS

Dozens of bus tours are available in Scotland. Gray Line (www.graylinetours.com) and Glasgow-based Scottish Tours (www.scottishtours.co.uk) offer three-, two- and one-day tours to places like St Andrews,

Loch Lomond, Loch Ness, the Borders and other destinations. All tours can be booked through the tourist information offices in Glasgow. Tour operators, centres, and hotels provide package holidays for sports such as golf and other outdoor sports.

Glasgow has a number of city hop-on-hop-off bus tours. Tours originate at George Square (www.cityxplora.com/locations/glasgow). Details of guides and tours can also be had from The Secretary, Scottish Tour Guides Association, Norrie's House, 18b Broad Street, Stirling, FK8 1EF, tel: 01786-447784; www.stga.co.uk. Members of this association wear official badges engraved with their names.

H

HEALTH AND MEDICAL CARE

Scotland, home of much pioneering work in medicine, is proud of the high standard of its health care. Medical care is free for EU (on production of the EHIC card) and Commonwealth residents under the National Health Service (NHS), at least until Brexit, after which point it may change. Other nationals should check to be sure they have adequate health insurance coverage. US residents should be aware that Medicare does not apply outside the United States.

Emergency care. A major hospital with 24-hour emergency service is: Glasgow Royal Infirmary, tel: 0141-211 4000.

Pharmacies. In Glasgow and a few other major urban areas you should find a duty chemist (drugstore) open until 9pm; otherwise, contact a police station for help in filling in an emergency prescription, or dial 999. Tourist Information Offices can advise you of the on-duty chemist in your area.

Insects. In the summer midges are a nuisance or worse, especially on Scotland's west coast. Clegs (horse flies) and tiny but devilish berry bugs also attack in warmer weather. Insect repellents aren't always effective; ask the advice of a chemist. Smidge is often the locally-preferred insect repellent.

L

LANGUAGE

Gaelic and old Scottish words and phrases in everyday use will baffle the most fluent English speaker. Today just over 60,000 Scots speak Gaelic, most of them residents of the Western Isles. English spoken with a strong Scots accent can take a while to get used to and place names are often not pronounced the way you'd expect: Kirkcudbright is *Kircoobree*, Culzean is *Cullane*, Colquhoun is *Cohoon*, Culross is *Coorus*, Menzies is *Mingies*, Wemyss is *Weems*. Here are some examples to help you along:

Scottish/Gaelic **English**
aber **river mouth**
ben **mountain**
bide a wee **wait a bit**
biggin **building**
brae **hillside**
bramble **blackberry**
brig **bridge**
burn **stream**
cairn **pile of stones as landmark**
ceilidh **song/story gathering**
clachan **hamlet**
croft **small land-holding**
dinna fash yersel' **don't get upset**
eilean **island**
fell **hill**
firth **estuary**
gait **street**
ghillie **attendant to hunting or fishing**

glen **valley**
haud yer wheesht **shut up**
inver **mouth of river**
ken **know**
kirk **church**
kyle **strait, narrows**
lang may yer lum reek **long may your chimney smoke (i.e. may you have a long life)**
link **dune**
linn **waterfall**
loch **lake**
mickle **small amount**
mull **promontory**
ness **headland**
provost **mayor**
sett **tartan pattern**
skirl **shriek of bagpipes**
strath **river valley**
thunderplump **thunderstorm**
tollbooth **old courthouse/jail**
wynd **lane, alley**

LGBTQ TRAVELLERS

Scotland is a conservative country and the LGBTQ scene is found primarily in Edinburgh and Glasgow; both have lively LGBTQ pubs and nightclubs. Support is offered by the LGBTQ Helpline Scotland (tel: 0300-123 2523; www.lgbthealth.org.uk/services-support/helpline/). The monthly magazine *Scotsgay* has a useful website (www.scotsgay.co.uk). There are two big LGBTQ events in the city each year, Pride Glasgow (https://prideglasgow.com) in August, and Glasgay! (http://outspokenarts.org) in late October to November.

M

MAPS

Free maps and helpful directions are available at any tourism office. For driving, a good map is essential. The Collins *Touring Map of Scotland* is published in association with VisitScotland. Collins also publishes illustrated street maps of Glasgow and the *A–Z Street Atlas* is available too. Route maps for hiking and biking are available from the tourist office; you may also want to buy one of the series of excellent ordinance survey (OS) maps that are available, especially for hiking.

MEDIA

Television. Viewers in Scotland have plenty of choice with two main BBC channels and digital television services providing a wide range of extra channels. Many larger hotels offer a variety of cable and satellite TV channels and pay-per-view films.

Radio. Radio Scotland is the main BBC radio service and national BBC radio stations also operate in Scotland. A range of commercial radio stations cater for different areas of Scotland. Various international stations can also be received.

Newspapers and magazines. In addition to British national newspapers, Scottish daily papers are: the *Herald* (published in Glasgow), the *Scotsman* (published in Edinburgh), the *Daily Record*, and the *Aberdeen Press and Journal*. Details of events and entertainment in and around Glasgow are given in the magazine *The List* (www.list.co.uk), published every two months. *The New York Times International Edition* and US weekly news magazines are sold in the major centres and at airports.

MONEY

Currency. The pound sterling (£) is a decimal monetary unit and is divided into 100 pence (p). Coins consist of 1p, 2p, 5p, 10p, 20p, 50p, £1 and £2; and banknotes consist of £1 (a few Scottish notes are still in circulation), £5, £10, £20, £50, and £100.

Scottish banks issue their own notes, which are not, technically, legal tender in England and Wales, although many shops will accept them and English banks will readily change them for you.

Currency exchange. You will get the best exchange rate for your foreign currency at banks (see Opening hours); currency exchange bureaux rarely offer as good a rate, and you'll get the worst rate at your hotel. Many Tourist Information Offices have currency exchange facilities.

Credit cards. Major credit cards are widely accepted in hotels, restaurants, petrol stations and shops, although not always in small guesthouses and B&Bs – signs are usually displayed indicating which are accepted.

Travellers' cheques. Travellers' cheques are still accepted throughout Scotland, although their use is in decline. You'll need your passport when cashing them, and banks will charge a fee. The American Express office will cash its own travellers' cheques without a fee.

O

OPENING HOURS

Opening hours may vary from place to place. However, banks are usually open Monday–Friday 9am–5pm, with branches in city centres open on Saturday mornings. Banks in small towns may close for lunch. Some rural areas are served only by mobile banks that arrive at regular intervals and stay for a few hours.

Offices and businesses are usually open Monday–Friday 9am–5pm; some have Saturday hours.

Post offices are open Monday–Friday 9am–5.30pm and Saturday 9am–12.30pm. Sub-stations have a half-day closing on Wednesday or Thursday.

Shop hours are normally Monday–Saturday 9am–5.30pm, some until 7pm or 8pm on Thursday. Some shops in villages and smaller towns close on Sunday and may close for lunch. In the larger cities in major shopping areas, shops open at either 11am or noon on Sunday and close at 5pm or 5.30pm.

Museums and sightseeing attractions have greatly varying opening hours. As a rule, attractions are open from about 10am until late afternoon, or early evening in summer. In winter many castles and other places of interest are closed to the public or open for limited periods. It's best to check online or call for information. Major **tourist information offices** are open all year round, usually Monday–Saturday 9am–6pm and Sunday 10am–4pm.

P

POLICE

Scottish police do not carry guns. Police patrol cars usually have yellow stripes and a blue light.

The emergency telephone number for police aid is **999** all over the country. You can also dial 0 and ask for the police.

POST OFFICES

Letters and packages sent within the UK can use the first- or second-class postal service. Because second-class mail may be slow, it's advisable to pay the modest extra postage for first class. Postcards and letters to Europe and elsewhere overseas automatically go by airmail. The post office offers an express mail service, Parcelforce Worldwide.

Stamps are sold at post offices (found in almost every Scottish village even if they share space with grocery shops) and newsagents, as well as from vending machines. Postboxes are red and come in many shapes and sizes. Glasgow's main post office is at 136 W Nile Street.

Postage. Within the UK from 70p first class; to Europe and the rest of world, airmail from £1.35p.

PUBLIC HOLIDAYS

Bank holidays in Scotland are not always closing days for offices and shops. Many towns have their individual holidays, generally on a Monday. VisitScotland publishes an annual list of local and national holidays and the chart below is a guide to fixed holidays. If one falls on a Saturday or Sunday, it is usual to take off the following Monday.

1 January **New Year's Day**
2 January **Bank Holiday**
25 December **Christmas Day**
26 December **Boxing Day**
   Moveable dates:
March or April **Good Friday/Easter Monday**
May **Spring Bank Holiday**
August **Summer Bank Holiday**

T

TELEPHONES

With the ubiquity of mobiles, there are fewer public phone boxes/kiosks. Those remaining are located in pubs, restaurants, post offices, shops and in the street. BT booths can usually accept coins, phonecards or credit/debit cards. Internet kiosks are also available. Phonecards of various denominations can be purchased from newsagents, post offices and tourist information offices. Some phones in small towns and public buildings are still coin-operated only.

Public phone booths display information on overseas dialling codes and the international exchange. Dial 118 505 for international directory inquiries, 155 for an international operator. Local directory enquiries are provided by several companies - numbers include 118 500, 118 365, 118 212 and 118 118, and for operator assistance, dial 100. Note that all 118 services are very expensive. To make a local reverse-charge call, dial 100 and ask the operator to reverse the charges.

Mobile (cell) phone coverage is not as good in Scotland as the rest of the UK, with rural areas particularly neglected by service providers. Glasgow, however, has good coverage, including 4G. Coverage varies extensively between different mobile phone companies. You will need a GSM cellular phone for use in Scotland. It is possible to rent these but this is an expensive option, especially for a short stay. If you have a GSM phone the roaming charges may well be high. The cheapest option is to buy a local UK SIM card to use in the GSM phone; incoming calls will be free and local calls inexpensive. Check out all the options before travelling.

TIME ZONES

Scotland, like the rest of the United Kingdom, is on Greenwich Mean Time. Between April and October clocks are put forward one hour.

New York	**Glasgow**	Jo'burg	Sydney	Auckland
7am	**noon**	1pm	9pm	11pm

TIPPING

While tipping is customary in Scotland, it's not mandatory. Hotels and restaurants may add a service charge to your bill, in which case tipping is not necessary. If service is not included, add about 10 percent to your bill. Many cafés and informal restaurants have a box for tips beside the cash register.

Tip hotel porters about £1 per bag, and tip your hotel maid about £5 per week. Lavatory attendants should get 20–50p. Your taxi driver will be pleased with 10 percent, and so will your tour guide, unless it's a free tour, when it's up to you. Hairdressers should get 10–20 percent.

TOURIST INFORMATION

There is probably no tourist destination in the world that produces more information for visitors than Scotland. Strategically placed throughout the Lowlands, Highlands and Islands are some 50 VisitScotland (www.visitscotland.com) tourist information centres, offering a wide range of publications, free or for sale, as well as expert advice. They're identified by purple signs with an iCentre in white.

In Glasgow, the information centre is at 156/158 Buchanan Street; tel: 0141-466 4083. National tourist information can be supplied by any major tourist information centre in Scotland. For further information on Scotland and the rest of Britain check www.visitbritain.com. In London you can drop into the City of London Visitor Centre, St Paul's Church-yard, London EC4M 8BY; tel: 020-7332 1456.

TRANSPORT

Scotland's extensive public transport network can be of considerable use to tourists. If you're touring the north without a car, a Travelpass enables you to travel on most coaches, trains and ferries operating in the Highlands and Islands at a significant saving. Maps, timetables and brochures are available free from tourist offices and transport termi-nals. There are also money-saving excursions, weekend and island-to-island ferry schemes.

City transport. Glasgow has good bus services, with some night buses also running. The main bus company is First Bus (www.firstgroup.com/greater-glasgow); contact the Travel Centre at Buchanan bus station, Killermont Street.

Glasgow also has a simple but efficient subway system, nicknamed 'the Clockwork Orange', which operates in the city centre run by SPT (www.spt.co.uk). The Park and Ride scheme involves parking your car at certain underground stations on the outskirts of the city and then taking the subway into the centre.

Coaches. Comfortable and rapid long-distance coaches with toilets link the major towns. For details, call **National Express** (tel: 0871-781 8181; www.nationalexpress.com); **Scottish Citylink** (tel: 0871-266 3333; www.citylink.co.uk) or **Buchanan Street Bus Station** (tel: 0141-333 3708). Citylink offers the Explorer Pass for three days' travel out of five, five days' travel out of ten or eight days out of 16 day, good on both major and local routes.

Trains. Train services include the InterCity trains, with the principal route from London Euston to Glasgow's Central Station (5 hours); there are day and night trains. From Glasgow's Queen Street Station, routes continue on to Perth, Dundee, Aberdeen and Inverness and there are smaller, secondary lines. For **National Rail Enquiries**, call 0845-748 4950 or visit www.nationalrail.co.uk.

Ferries. Ferries to the Western Isles are generally run by **Caledonian MacBrayne** (tel: 0800-066 5000; www.calmac.co.uk). There are also many ferries between the islands. Reservations are essential in peak season for the more popular car ferries.

Taxis. In Glasgow you'll find most taxis are the black, London-style cabs. A taxi's yellow 'For Hire' sign is lit when it's available for hire. There are taxi ranks at airports and stations, and you can hail them on the street. Many hotels also have a button you can press, which automatically calls a taxi to the front door. Major centres have 24-hour radio taxi services. There's an extra charge for luggage. If you hire a taxi for a long-distance trip, negotiate the price with the driver before setting off.

TRAVELLERS WITH DISABILITIES

Capability Scotland is Scotland's leading disability organisation, providing a range of flexible services which support disabled people of all ages in their everyday lives. Contact: Capability Scotland, Osborne House, 1 Osborne Terrace, Edinburgh EH12 5HG (tel: 0131-337 9076, www.capability-scotland.org.uk).

V

VISAS AND ENTRY REQUIREMENTS

For non-British citizens the same formalities apply at Scottish ports of entry as elsewhere in the UK. Citizens of EU countries need only an identity card, although this is liable to change once Brexit negotiations work out a new system of doing things. Be sure to check the latest updates before you travel. Visitors from the US and most Commonwealth countries need only a valid passport for stays of up to 6 months.

On arrival at a British port or airport, if you have goods to declare you follow the red channel; with nothing to declare you take the green route, bypassing inspection, although customs officers may make random spot checks. Free exchange of non-duty-free goods for personal use is permitted between EU countries and the UK. Duty-free items are still subject to restrictions: check before you go. There's no limit on the amount of currency you can bring into or take out of Britain.

W

WEBSITES AND INTERNET ACCESS
The following are some useful websites for planning your visit.

Tourism

www.visitscotland.com VisitScotland

www.visitbritain.com British Tourist Authority

www.glasgowlife.org.uk Runs most of the major museums in the city

https://peoplemakeglasgow.com Greater Glasgow and Clyde Valley

www.undiscoveredscotland.co.uk Undiscovered Scotland

www.scotland.org.uk Travel Scotland

www.list.co.uk *The List* events magazine online

www.glasgow.gov.uk Information from the local council

www.glasgowlive.co.uk The latest news and sport from the city

General

www.historicenvironment.scot Caring for and promoting Scotland's historic environment

www.nts.org.uk National Trust for Scotland

www.eventscotland.org Forthcoming festivals and sports events

www.scotsman.com *The Scotsman*

www.metoffice.gov.uk Find out the latest weather reports and help plan your day

Glasgow is well connected when it comes to internet access, with even some of the remotest locations supported by dial-up, broadband or even Wi-fi. It's highly unlikely you'll find a hotel, guest house or B&B

that doesn't offer free wireless internet access. Public libraries across Scotland offer free internet access and airports have computers available to access the internet, as well as Wi-fi hotspots.

Y

YOUTH HOSTELS

Hostelling Scotland runs around 70 hostels. Visitors can stay without being members of the association but membership brings many benefits, including reduced prices for rooms. Their address is 7 Glebe Crescent, Stirling FK8 2JA (tel: 01786-891 400 or 0345-293 7373 for reservations; www.syha.org.uk). Hostels are graded by the VisitScotland quality assurance scheme.

RECOMMENDED HOTELS

Accommodation is ubiquitous in central Glasgow and gets less prevalent the further one drifts from the main train stations. The options cover a wide spectrum, from the basic B&B (bed-and-breakfast) to modern world-class luxury hotels. VisitScotland (www.visitscotland.com) publishes brochures and booklets detailing available accommodation, prices, facilities, etc.

Below you will find a selection of accommodation chosen for its quality and value for money. Prices are based on two people sharing a double room in high season with breakfast and VAT included. Keep in mind that prices vary according to time of year and availability. All rooms have bath or shower and all establishments take major credit cards unless otherwise indicated. Glasgow is extremely busy during the summer, so book well in advance if you plan to visit during that period. Although head into a VisitScotland office for a lifeline if you arrive in the city with no reservation to find lots of 'no vacancy' signs.

££££	over £250
£££	£150–£250
££	£100–£150
£	below £100

CENTRAL GLASGOW & MERCHANT CITY

ABode Glasgow ££ *129 Bath St, tel: 0141-221 6789, www.abodeglasgow.co.uk.* Located in an elegant Edwardian building, *ABode's* rooms come in four categories, ranging from 'Comfortable' to 'Fabulous'; the main difference between them is size and the odd extra (for example, Nespresso machines), though nearly all feature printed wallpaper, picture frame headboards and tartan spreads, while a few rooms retain original wood-panelled walls and stained-glass windows. 59 rooms.

Babbity Bowster £ *16–18 Blackfriars St, off High St, tel: 0141-552 5055, www.babbitybowster.com.* Best known as a pub, *Babbity Bowster* also features five plain but serviceable rooms (singles and doubles) that provide visitors with a great, and decently priced, Merchant City location; a simple breakfast is included. 5 rooms.

Brunswick Hotel £ *108 Brunswick St, tel: 0141-552 0001*, www.brunswick hotel.co.uk. In the heart of the Merchant City quarter, this stylish hotel is extremely good value in terms of both location and elegance. Standard rooms on the higher levels are less prone to the traffic noise. There's also an on-site café-bar open seven days a week. 26 rooms.

Carlton George £££ *44 West George St, G2 1DH, tel: 0141-353 6373*, www.carlton.nl/george. A modern, luxurious, state-of-the-art hotel in the heart of Glasgow next to Queen Street train station. Some rooms include access to the executive lounge, with complimentary coffee, tea and soft drinks in the day, and free wine, beer and spirits each evening. *The Windows* rooftop restaurant offers excellent Scottish cooking and great views. 64 rooms.

citizenM ££ *60 Renfrew St, tel: 0203-519 1111*, www.citizenm.com. This modern European chain offers a luxury experience that won't break the bank; check in via computer then head to your room to enjoy the innovative mood lighting, hip decor and rain shower. After that, you could do a lot worse than hang around in the cool *canteenM*, a homely breakfast bar-meets-lounge area that's open round the clock. Breakfast can be added on. 198 rooms.

The Grand Central Hotel £££ *99 Gordon St, tel: 0141-240 3700*, www.phcompany.com. Having enjoyed extensive refurbishments in 2018, *The Grand Central* is one of Glasgow's landmark hotels, set inside an old Victorian building that forms part of Glasgow Central train station. Luminaries such as Winston Churchill and Frank Sinatra have stayed here. 186 rooms.

Grasshoppers Hotel ££ *87 Union St, tel: 0141-222 2666*, www.grass hoppersglasgow.com. Penthouse rooms above an office building close to historic Glasgow Central station give great city views. Oak flooring, bespoke, Scandinavian-style furnishings and pod-like bathrooms are found in the rooms. It's surprisingly quiet here for its central location, and the friendly staff and wholesome breakfast make this a charming city experience. 30 rooms.

Hotel Indigo £££ *75 Waterloo St, tel: 0141-226 7700,* http://ihg.com/hotel indigo/. Within this 19th-century sandstone building is a 21st-century hotel, with modern, stylish rooms, elegant floral themes and warm tones. There's a fitness studio on site, which might come in handy after the decadence of hotel's restaurant and cocktail lounge. 94 rooms.

ibis Styles Centre West ££ *116 Waterloo St, tel: 0141-428 4477,* www.accorhotels.com. For the musically-inclined, there are plenty of little gems built into the interiors here, including drum cymbal light shades, old LPs, and homages in the bathrooms to all the bands that have emanated from Glasgow. Rooms are minimalist but comfortable enough. 137 rooms.

Jurys Inn Glasgow £ *80 Jamaica St, tel: 0141-314 4800,* www.jurysinns.com. A vast hotel overlooking Glasgow Central station that has modern rooms that are kept clean and neat. There's a bar, restaurant and room service, but it's the location that is the main selling point. 321 rooms.

Kimpton Blythswood Square Hotel ££££ *11 Blythswood Square, tel: 0141-248 8888,* www.kimptonblythswoodsquare.com. Luxury hotel boasting gorgeous Georgian architecture, with smartly renovated rooms and an on-site spa. The neighbourhood restaurant *Bo & Birdy* features farm-to-table cooking, while the hotel offers indulgent afternoon teas. 113 rooms.

Malmaison ££ *278 West George St, tel: 0141-378 0384,* www.malmaison.com. Modern and trendy with beautifully decorated rooms, this former Greek Orthodox church still manages to preserve its important historical character. Vaulted cellar restaurant serving Scottish flavours with a French influence. Breakfast can be added on. 72 rooms.

Moxy ££ *210 High St, tel: 0141-846 0256,* www.moxy-hotels.marriott.com. Playful and energetic, this place would score highly on a budget-savvy millennial-traveller's checklist: flat-screen TVs, ultrafast Wi-fi and an edgy, urban location – it's just east of the city centre. The rooms are compact but the communal space is where the action is: a buzzing area with a central bar, long communal tables dotted with coffee-table books, and a pool and table football table. 181 rooms.

Native Glasgow ££ *14 St Vincent Place, tel: 020-7313 3886,* www.native places.com. The first thing that impresses upon you about *Native Glasgow* is the building. The beautiful Edwardian facade once belonged to the Anchor Line Shipping Company and the 1920s ocean liner theme continues within at the *Anchor Line Restaurant*. This aparthotel's rooms employ more modern luxuries, however, with cooking facilities and seating areas adding extra comfort and convenience. 64 apartments.

Pipers' Tryst ££ *30–34 McPhater St, tel: 0141-353 5551,* www.thepiping centre.co.uk. Attached to the National Piping Centre, set back from the main road in the heart of Glasgow, the eight decently sized rooms feature decor that is firmly on the side of cheery tartan. There are cheaper rates for single occupancy, tremendously helpful staff and a wholesome breakfast to see you on your way. 8 rooms.

Radisson Blu Hotel £££ *301 Argyle St, tel: 0141-204 3333,* www.radisson blu.co.uk/hotel glasgow. Around the corner from Glasgow Central station, this hotel has a jaw-dropping glass-fronted lobby that is likely to impress anyone interested in contemporary design. The cavernous art-filled atrium bar is a social hub, while the *Collage Corner Bar* and restaurant has picked up awards. Standard modern rooms can seem a tad dull, but the corner suites are gorgeous. 91 rooms.

Z Hotel £ *36 North Frederick St, tel: 0141-212 4550,* www.thezhotels.com. The handsome, sandstone facade of this former printworks conceals compact but fabulously sleek rooms, minimally furnished (there are few tables and chairs to speak of, and TVs are embedded in the wall), with sparkling wet rooms boxed off by glass partitions. The unfailingly helpful staff conspire to make this a terrific place to spend a night or two. Breakfast not included. 104 rooms.

THE WEST END & CLYDE

Alamo Guest House ££ *46 Gray St, tel: 0141-339 2395,* www.alamoguest house.com. Good-value, family-run boarding house next to Kelvingrove Park, with ten rooms, each one completely different in size and character, variously featuring stucco plasterwork, French oak beds, slate-tile sinks and cast-iron chandeliers, or perhaps a freestanding tub. 10 rooms.

Amadeus Guesthouse £ *411 North Woodside Rd, tel: 0141-339 8257,* www. amadeusguesthouse.co.uk. Handy West End Location just steps away from Kelvinbridge subway station. This welcoming, family-friendly Victorian townhouse offers stylish, individually decorated boutique style bedrooms, and a lovely continental breakfast. 6 rooms.

Argyll Guest House £ *970 Sauchiehall St, tel: 0141-357 5155,* www.argyll guesthouseglasgow.co.uk. Near Kelvingrove Park and art galleries, this small, friendly hotel is a good budget option where the staff are very helpful. Scottish style buffet breakfasts are available, and served the sister hotel, *The Argyll*, across the street. 18 rooms.

Crowne Plaza Glasgow ££ *Congress Rd, tel: 0871-942 9091,* www.ihg. com/crowneplaza. Modern high-rise beside the Clyde and the SEC, offering a range of functional rooms and suites, a grand reception with bar-restaurant, a shop, and pool. 283 rooms.

Hilton Garden Inn ££ *Finnieston Quay, tel: 0141-240 1002,* http://hilton gardeninn3.hilton.com. A stylish yet comfortable place to stay next to the Clyde, with a fresh contemporary design and beguiling café-bar with views of the river from the terrace. Great for attending events at SSE Hydro or conferences at the SEC. 164 rooms.

Hostelling Scotland Glasgow Youth Hostel £ *8 Park Terrace, tel: 0141-332 3004,* www.hostellingscotland.org.uk. Popular but surprisingly low-key hostel located in a wonderful townhouse in one of the West End's grandest terraces. All the dorms (singles up to eight-bed shared rooms) are en-suite and there are plenty of private rooms available too.

Other facilities include common area, self-catering kitchen and laundry. 110 beds.

Hotel du Vin & Bistro £££ *1 Devonshire Gardens, tel: 0141-378 0385,* www.hotelduvin.com. In a leafy west-Glasgow district, this luxury boutique hotel occupies a stunning Victorian terrace and offers beautifully decorated rooms and impeccable service. Rooms typically feature large open-plan seating areas, Bose sound systems and monsoon power showers, and there's further decadence courtesy of the cigar room and whisky bar. 49 rooms.

Kelvin Hotel £ *15 Buckingham Terrace, tel: 0141-339 7143,* www.kelvin hotel.com. Family-owned hotel in an impressive Victorian building in the West End. Decorated in soft pastels, the guest rooms have high ceilings and free Wi-fi. A fully fitted communal kitchen is available to guests. 21 rooms.

Queensgate Apartments ££ *107 Dowanhill St, tel: 077-9665 1451,* www. queensgateapartments.com. Attractive and cosy apartments, a short walk from cosmopolitan Byres Road and Glasgow University, with their own private entrance to an Edwardian West End townhouse. They sleep up to four in two large double bedrooms and have a spacious dining kitchen. 2 apartments.

Village Hotel Glasgow ££ *7 Festival Gate, Pacific Quay, tel: 0141-375 3202,* www.village-hotels.co.uk. Opened in 2015, this hotel offers everything you could want under one roof, at extremely good value. The very on-trend bedrooms feature super-comfy beds. Other facilities include an indoor pool, gym and pub dining. 120 rooms.

SOUTHSIDE

10 Hotel ££ *10–16 Queen's Dr, tel: 0141-424 0160,* www.10hotel.co.uk. In a great location with views over Queen's Park, this graceful Victorian building has stylish interiors that fluently combine fashionable design with original features. The chic restaurant offers classic cooking with a modern twist. 26 rooms.

Glasgow Guest House £ *56 Dumbrek Rd, near Pollok Park, tel: 0141-427 0129*, www.glasgow-guest-house.co.uk. This bed and breakfast offers homely accommodation and is handy for access to the parks, particularly Bellahouston. and Pollok Country Park. The owners are lovely and helpful. 7 rooms.

Mar Hall Golf and Spa Resort ££££ *Earl of Mar Estate, Bishopton, Renfrew, tel: 0141-812 9999*, www.marhall.com. Stunning Gothic mansion within acres of woodland and with an 18-hole golf course, just 10 minutes west of Glasgow airport. Luxury rooms and suites have four-poster beds and come in calming hues. The Decléor Spa offers treatments and a swimming pool. 53 rooms.

Sherbrooke Castle Hotel £££ *11 Sherbrooke Ave, Pollokshields, tel: 0141-427 4227*, www.sherbrookecastlehotel.com. A Victorian mock-Gothic mansion complete with baronial turrets near Pollok Park. Tartan carpets, period furnishings and antiques give the public areas a cosy atmospheric feel, while guest rooms have modern bathrooms, warmth and some have four-poster beds. 18 rooms.

NORTH OF THE CITY

Cameron House Hotel ££££ *Loch Lomond, tel: 01389-310 777*, www.cameronhouse.co.uk. This five-star hotel is housed in a luxurious baronial-style mansion in a stunning Loch Lomond waterside setting. There are first-class spa and golf facilities, and you can even arrive by seaplane. 136 rooms.

Dakota Eurocentral £ *1–3 Parklands Ave, Eurocentral Business Park (off the A8/M8), tel: 01698-835 444*, http://eurocentral.dakotahotels.co.uk. A stylish yet cosy hotel with lots of contemporary design touches and free Wi-fi. The award-winning bar and grill serves excellent Scottish fish dishes and a good range of cocktails. 92 rooms.

INDEX

INSIGHT ◉ GUIDES POCKET GUIDE

GLASGOW

First Edition 2020

Editor: Tatiana Wilde
Author: Paul Stafford
Head of DTP and Pre-Press: Rebeka Davies
Managing Editor: Carine Tracanelli
Picture Editor: Aude Vauconsant
Picture Manager: Tom Smyth
Layout: Ruth Bradley
Cartography Update: Carte
Photography Credits: Credit: Kay Roxby / Alamy Stock Photo 7R; Credit: Scott Hortop Travel / Alamy Stock Photo 105; Getty Images 5MC, 6R, 13, 19, 21, 53, 84; iStock 4TC, 4MC, 4TL, 5TC, 5M, 5MC, 5M, 6L, 11, 15, 17, 24, 29, 30, 33, 35, 37, 39, 45, 46, 50, 57, 59, 62, 65, 66, 71, 73, 74, 79, 81, 87, 89, 90, 92, 94, 99, 101, 102; Shutterstock 1, 4ML, 5T, 7L, 23, 26, 41, 42, 49, 54, 61, 68, 76, 82
Cover Picture: Shutterstock

Distribution
UK, Ireland and Europe: Apa Publications (UK) Ltd; sales@insightguides.com
United States and Canada: Ingram Publisher Services; ips@ingramcontent.com
Australia and New Zealand: Woodslane; info@woodslane.com.au
Southeast Asia: Apa Publications (SN) Pte; singaporeoffice@insightguides.com
Worldwide: Apa Publications (UK) Ltd; sales@insightguides.com

Special Sales, Content Licensing and CoPublishing
Insight Guides can be purchased in bulk quantities at discounted prices. We can create special editions, personalised jackets and corporate imprints tailored to your needs. sales@insightguides.com; www.insightguides.biz

All Rights Reserved
© 2020 Apa Digital (CH) AG and Apa Publications (UK) Ltd

Printed in China

No part of this book may be reproduced, stored in a retrieval system or transmitted in any form or means electronic, mechanical, photocopying, recording or otherwise, without prior written permission from Apa Publications.

Contact us
Every effort has been made to provide accurate information in this publication, but changes are inevitable. The publisher cannot be responsible for any resulting loss, inconvenience or injury. We would appreciate it if readers would call our attention to any errors or outdated information. We also welcome your suggestions; please contact us at: hello@insightguides.com
www.insightguides.com